Classics

CRYSTAL PALACE

FOOTBALL CLUB

GLAZIERS' GREAT VICTORY.
Crystal Palace, 1; Newcastle, 0.

TAKING GOALS TO NEWCASTLE.
Knocked out in the First Round.   A Gh-ASTLEY Affair.

Here's how Crystal Palace and their fans celebrated the glorious FA Cup victory over Newcastle in 1907. The match is the first featured in this book. Notice the play on the name of the Palace scorer, Horace Astley – no doubt every memory of the occasion was indeed ghastly for Tyneside folk!

Classics

CRYSTAL PALACE
FOOTBALL CLUB

REV. NIGEL SANDS

TEMPUS

That goal! Terry Long's shot rockets into the Real Madrid net. See page 41 to relish the occasion further!

First published 2002

Tempus Publishing Limited
The Mill, Brimscombe Port,
Stroud, Gloucestershire, GL5 2QG

British Library Cataloguing in Publication Data.
A catalogue record for this book is available from the British Library.

ISBN 0 7524 2733 4

Typesetting and origination by Tempus Publishing Limited
Printed in Great Britain by Midway Colour Print, Wiltshire

Chairman's Foreword

As Crystal Palace FC stands poised to break into the most senior echelon of football in our country, it is good to see our club continuing to produce top quality merchandise for our fans to enjoy alongside the experience of watching and supporting our team.

Therefore I am again pleased to offer a few words of endorsement at the start of another book from the pen of our loyal honorary chaplain. The hundred great Palace matches which follow are bound to rekindle the memories of us all at some point, while the whole volume is of a quality which does justice to Crystal Palace – our tradition, our reputation and our aspirations for future success.

Simon Jordan
Chairman, Crystal Palace FC

Preface

It is a pleasure again to be able to offer a book about Crystal Palace FC to our supporters for them to enjoy and I'm confident that the combination of my writing, the brilliant pictures and the clever editorial work of Tempus Publishing will produce a volume which Eagles fans will welcome. I also know that many of them will keep it with its predecessors to help to build a really comprehensive library of Palace-based publications.

Every Palace book I've written has produced a flurry of correspondence from other Eagles folk to do with the content, or, sometimes, wider matters to do with our club. The last one, *Crystal Palace 100 Greats*, was no exception, but those who wrote to chide me over my selection may be interested to know twelve months later that they were substantially outnumbered by those who simply approved the choices and had enjoyed them. That said, I can't think that there will be much discussion over the matches I've selected here – depending upon the ages of our readers, everyone will have relished some of these games, some a lot of them, a few most of them. Surely no-one, now, has seen all of them? I'd be delighted to hear from someone who can prove me wrong!

If there is one mild disappointment in my mind at the time of penning this preface, it lies in the fact that we are short of a string of recent Palace games that could seriously be claimed to have been 'classic'. Like every Palace fan, I long for that to be rectified as soon as possible.

Finally, as always, Palace supporters who want to discuss particular or general matters raised in this book are most welcome to do so. Please write to me at Wickham Rectory, Newbury, Berkshire, RG20 8HD and be kind enough to enclose a SAE for a prompt reply.

Nigel Sands
Wickham
September 2002

Acknowledgements

Once again, like virtually every modern publication from our football club, this book is indebted to the photographers who produced the pictures that accompany the text, and especially among them Neil Everitt. Neil has been our club photographer for nearly thirty years and if his contribution to our club is often unsung, our loyal fans know just how fortunate we are to have his talent at our club's disposal and available for our pleasure. I am also particularly grateful to Paul Firmage, who found one picture for this book, the subject of which had defeated everyone else.

Equally, the kind and conscientious help of two other friends of mine has added detail and therefore enhanced credibility to this book because David Keats and Tony Bowden found the times of several substitutions which were only available in some pretty remote places. Colin Duncan provided his specialist talent as a proof reader and so, again, everybody is indebted to him.

Our publishing 'team' at Tempus should also be thanked: with every Palace book they publish for us, they grow closer to the indefinable but unique ethos that is Crystal Palace FC.

Finally, it is always possible in a volume like this, that a photograph which was used in a previous club publication has been reproduced here without accurate acknowledgement. Care has been taken to avoid this, but if it were to be discovered, please accept the author's apologies and let him know so that proper recognition may be given in later editions.

What makes a match classic?

Among my prefatory remarks in the previous volume in this continuing sequence of books to do with Crystal Palace FC, I offered a short piece which gave considered thought to the concept of 'greatness' as it applied to footballers, who were, after all, the subject matter of that book. Several readers, not all of them Palace folk by any means, told me that they appreciated that discussion, the like of which apparently is not to be found in the parallel publications in that particular series from other clubs.

So, the questions before author and readers at the start of this book become what we actually mean by a classic when the word is applied to football matches – what makes a match a 'classic'?

It is not enough to simply say that a game where our club scores a lot of goals must be a great one. It might be, but, on its own, sheer numbers of goals won't be a sufficient criterion. Rather, the quality of the opposition; the significance of the result (in terms perhaps of club records or its future destiny); the occasion itself; these are all factors which will contribute towards the greatness of a particular match, as are its historic significance, the manner in which goals are scored, maybe their timing and by whom.

Thus, it will be possible to find in the following pages a clutch of matches which our beloved club didn't manage to win! Or, indeed, even draw! There's even one in which the Palace didn't play!

Of course, a classic football match depends to some degree upon its status, and its setting, not to mention the number of fans it attracts, although, equally, everyone will agree that many of the games that are billed as the biggest of the season (of which there are on average some three or four a term!) fail to come anywhere near to being 'classic' within our meaning of the word.

BY THE SAME AUTHOR

Images of Sport – Crystal Palace Football Club
    (Published 1999)
Crystal Palace Football Club – 100 Greats
    (Published 2001)

Crystal Palace Roll of Honour

FA PREMIERSHIP:	Best Season:	Third place in 1990/91
FOOTBALL LEAGUE:	Division One:	Champions 1993/94 Promoted via play-offs 1996/97
	Second Division:	Champions 1978/79 Runners-up 1968/69
	Third Division:	Runners-up 1963/64
	Third Division (South):	Champions 1920/21 Runners-up 1928/29 1930/31; 1938/39
	Fourth Division:	Runners-up 1960/61
FA CUP:		Runners-up 1989/90
FOOTBALL LEAGUE CUP:		Semi-finalists 1992/93; 1994/95;2000/01
FULL MEMBERS' CUP:		Winners 1990/91
MOST CAPPED PLAYER:	Eric Young	19 caps for Wales as a Crystal Palace player
MOST LEAGUE APPS:	Jim Cannon	571 (1973-88)
MOST LEAGUE GOALS IN CLUB CAREER:	Peter Simpson	153 (1929-36)

Saturday 12 January 1907
Referee: Mr A.G. Hines

FA Challenge Cup (Old) First Round
Attendance: 28,000

The Crystal Palace club had only been in existence for something less than eighteen months before it secured this brilliant, first, major shock result and it seems entirely appropriate that this selection of a hundred classic Crystal Palace matches should begin at Gallowgate on a cold midwinter's afternoon in 1907.

Frankly, I believe that this victory should still be regarded as Palace's greatest of all – so far, of course! – given the relative status of the two outfits. Palace were still in their infancy and possessed a matter of just four months experience in the First Division of the Southern League. The contrast could scarcely have been more pronounced because Newcastle were among the foremost sides in the country throughout the first decade of the twentieth century. They were the current Football League champions and had been FA Cup finalists the previous season; they were unbeaten at home for more than a year and fielded several current internationals in their line-up. Regarded by the contemporary pundits as the perfect football team, The Magpies were favourites to win this clash by the biggest margin of the round!

Perhaps Palace's greatest asset in this tie was that a number of the team, like Horace Astley, winger Charlie Wallace and goalkeeper Bob Hewitson, hailed from the North-East; skipper Wilfred Innerd had actually played for Newcastle teams, as had Dick Harker and outside left 'Dickie' Roberts.

It was inevitable that the Palace would have to endure a lot of Newcastle pressure and this they did successfully. However, just as half-time approached the seemingly impossible occurred when Horace Astley eluded the converging full-backs, then raced on to a return pass from George Woodger and thumped a terrific shot past the bemused Scottish international goalkeeper Jimmy Lawrence to give the Palace the lead. And nothing Newcastle could offer after the break could retrieve the situation! In fact, incredibly, the margin could even have been greater! George Woodger was twice denied by Lawrence, then lifted a third opportunity over the bar – and Palace finished with only ten men after Charlie Ryan had to be carried off ten minutes before the end!

A little girl called Lucy wrote a poem about this famous win which finished:

'Mark my word my friends, I'll bet,
That the Palace will win the 'Tin Pot' yet'.

We're still hoping so, Lucy, nearly a hundred years later, but maybe some of today's readers of your lovely poem will be able to cheer them when they do!

Horace Astley.

Newcastle 0

Crystal Palace 1
Astley

CRYSTAL PALACE v. WOLVERHAMPTON WANDERERS

Thursday 21 January 1909
Referee: unknown

FA Challenge Cup (Old) First Round Replay
Attendance: 12,300

Crystal Palace had already created something of a surprise in the football world of the day by holding the Wolverhampton giants, who were the FA Cup holders, to a 2-2 draw at their Molineux headquarters on the previous Saturday. However, the prospect of them repeating the feat, let alone improving upon it in the replay, was considered remote. And that sensible viewpoint was confirmed when the visitors netted inside the first minute through their centre forward.

Fortunately, Palace were able to make the speedy response that was required on the heavy, liberally sanded turf when our amateur inside forward Billy Lawrence took a pass from former Tottenham star John Brearley, rounded full back Collins and shot firmly past the exposed goalkeeper. But, again, matters appeared to be going against the Palace early in the second half when our defender Ted Collins was hurt, but he returned to the fray after treatment to play on the wing. Somewhere around the middle of the half Palace took the lead through our irrepressible right-winger George Garratt after fine work by Jimmy Bauchop. Wolves' star amateur, the Reverend Kenneth Hunt, who subsequently came to play for Crystal Palace, provided the opening for their equaliser; this was converted with eight minutes of normal time remaining by Radford after the Palace goalkeeper Joe Johnson had only been able to parry the greasy ball following a fierce shot from Hedley.

Extra time, in the fading light and on the now badly cut up pitch, produced such drama that no Palace fan who witnessed it could ever forget it. Palace forged ahead once more towards the end of the first period when Jimmy Bachop took full advantage of another superb pass from John Brearley, but it was in the dying moments of the match that Archie Needham scored one of the finest goals in all Palace history. He received the ball in the centre circle, inside the Palace half, and ran at the Wolves defence, striding through tackles as well as the strength-sapping mud, before lashing it into the net and falling exhausted in the Wolves penalty area and there accepting the acclaim of the fans and the congratulations of his team-mates. It was a wonderful goal, scored by a fine club servant who had been with the Palace from the very beginning, and Palace supporters who saw it were still reminiscing about it six or seven decades later!

LITTLE RED RIDING HOOD—Modern Version.
Or, keeping the Wolf from the Door.

This brilliant cartoon depicts the 1909 FA Cup defeat of Wolves.

Crystal Palace 4
Lawrence, Garratt
Bauchop, Needham

Wolves 2
Hedley
Radford

(after extra time)

Saturday 16 September 1911
Referee: Lieut. W.C. Clover

Southern League, First Division
Attendance: 8,000

Palace skipper Harry
Hanger heads for goal
against Swindon Town.

This book about classic Crystal Palace matches would not be complete without some account which related to the club's fortunes at the time when it was competing in the Southern League. Of course, a whole volume could be devoted to that period between 1905 and 1920 but – hopefully our readers will agree – just one game will suffice. In fact it is probably a typical Palace match from that era: it isn't a high-scoring drama, although the club were engaged in quite a lot of these; it doesn't come from a particularly successful League season, though Palace finished as runners-up in 1914; nor does it involve issues affecting a championship or promotion. It is quite simply a game which showed Palace for what they generally were in the Southern League – a strong team, respected by opponents and deserving of the admiration of their fans, but not actually a title-winning one.

The 1911/12 Southern League season was entering its third week and Palace, who had finished fourth the previous April, were at home to the champions Swindon Town. It was an attractive fixture in its own right, certainly for Palace supporters, but it took place during the Festival of Empire which was being staged at the Crystal Palace and this may have detrimentally affected the attendance. Truth to tell, the Palace side didn't play particularly well except for one spell after the interval, and the side demonstrated a lack of discipline which modern-day fans and management would find hard to forgive. Palace certainly lacked sparkle in the first half and Swindon deserved the lead they gained just before the break, but with a reshuffling of the inside forward trio for the restart, Palace became much more effective.

The Palace now started to play well and they dominated the next half hour, twice gaining reward when Dick Harker equalised on his return to Palace after an absence of four years playing in Scotland, and Charlie Hewitt put Palace ahead no more than a minute later. But the Palace players then made the gross error of easing up and Swindon were able to net an equaliser of their own in the closing stages. Probably Palace's best player on the day was skipper Harry Hanger who marked Harold Fleming so tightly that the brilliant England man was barely able to influence the proceedings, but Jimmy Hughes was also outstanding in Palace colours. In retrospect though, perhaps the most interesting Palace player to have taken part in this game was Charlie Woodhouse, who had been the club's top goalscorer the previous season. Charlie became ill after just 11 matches and 6 goals in 1911/12 and he died suddenly. He is buried in Elmers End cemetery (by Birkbeck station).

Crystal Palace 2
Harker
Hewitt

Swindon Town 2
Bown (2)

CRYSTAL PALACE v. SOUTHAMPTON

Tuesday 29 March 1921
Referee: unknown

Football League, Third Division
Attendance: 20,000

Given the extremely close challenge at the top of the newly formed Third Division of the Football League at Easter 1921, it may appear surprising to present day readers that this vital match against our closest rivals for the single promotion place allowed was not staged on the Good Friday bank holiday, but upon the Tuesday afternoon, by which time many of Palace's growing band of supporters had had to return to work. The reason the game had to be delayed lay in the original ownership of the land on which The Nest had been built around the turn of the century because the Ecclesiastical Commissioners (now the Church Commissioners) had stipulated to the new owners, the London, Brighton and South Coast Railway, that no matches were to be staged on their proposed football ground on either Good Friday or Christmas Day.

However, the advantage for those Palace fans who were able to attend the match was that it thus became the second of the 'paired' fixtures between Crystal Palace and Southampton, while the first one, at The Dell the previous day, had been drawn after Phil Bates had equalised for Palace with what was the last kick of the match. Now came the vital 'second leg' and it is a measure of Saints' calibre that they again led until the last few minutes, because Palace's home form at this time was outstanding with six victories in a row prior to this fixture.

The quality of the contest was excellent, especially if one considers the issue at stake. Saints' right winger gave them the lead in the first half and Palace were on the back foot until the break, but after the interval they mounted fabulous pressure. Nevertheless, it was only in the closing stages that Palace were able to equalise. A corner was hoofed away by Southampton but gathered by Palace's doughty current Welsh international J.T. Jones, who lobbed the ball back into the mêlée in front of the visitors' goal where Palace's tough little forward Alf Wood lashed it home.

Palace managed to retain the top spot as a result of this outcome and their points tally ran virtually parallel with that of Southampton in the remaining games, so that a big win over Northampton some four weeks later confirmed our championship and promotion, leaving Southampton to wait another twelve months for their own honours.

Alf Wood is seated on the far right of the front row in this 1920 Palace team photograph.

Crystal Palace 1
Wood

Southampton 1
Brown

CRYSTAL PALACE v. NOTTINGHAM FOREST

Saturday 27 August 1921
Referee: unknown

Football League, Second Division
Attendance: 20,000

When the Second Division fixtures for 1921/22 were announced, there was inevitably huge interest in their details among the supporters of Crystal Palace because the club had gained promotion the previous spring and were now poised to make their debut at this higher level. When it was discovered that Palace would begin their campaign with a home game against Nottingham Forest, the excitement became intense because, even if Forest had not fared too well in the Second Division in 1920/21, they were one of the glamour clubs of that section and had gained a lot of summer publicity even in the south of England by making several high profile close-season signings to augment a challenge for a much sought return to the top flight. The best known of their new men was the former Aston Villa, Liverpool and England goalkeeper Sam Hardy; Forest had also paid big money for three new forwards, all of whom lined up at The Nest against the Palace.

Palace had also entered the transfer market, but rather to deepen the pool of talent available to manager Edmund Goodman than to actually change the personnel or formation. Indeed, the Palace team that played in the club's first match in the higher divisions of the Football League was comprised entirely of men who had made major contributions to our success in the Third Division in 1920/21.

The Nest, however, had required some improvements in order to be able to cope with the demands of Second Division football. That tight, humble little ground underwent 'considerable alterations' in the summer of 1921, but several Second Division clubs still complained about the accommodation and facilities there, and these cannot have been enhanced by a fire in the grandstand during a London Challenge Cup tie against Charlton at the end of October. In fact, though, Second Division gates were to prove a little disappointing this season and the estimated 20,000 attendance for Forest's visit wasn't exceeded even in local derbies against Fulham and West Ham. Only the magic lure of the FA Cup pulled in more, when some 25,000 came for a tie against local rivals Millwall, from the Third Division.

What took place at The Nest on this warm, dry summer's afternoon probably represented Palace's best performance in the Second Division during their entire four-year tenure there between 1921 and 1925. Although Forest's craftsmen were able to respond to Palace's opener, they were hit by three more goals in fairly quick succession to which they had no substantive answer, so that by the end the home side were worthy and deserved winners and even Forest's renowned goalkeeper had been powerless to stem the tide.

Initially, as might perhaps have been expected, Forest were the better side and Palace's own goalkeeper, Jack Alderson, had to be in fine form but he positioned himself adroitly and handled cleanly. Then, a little after midway through the first half, Palace earned two quick corners on the left and from Albert Feebury's second delivery Palace's Welsh international star J.T. Jones netted with a spectacular, towering header which left poor Hardy rooted to the spot and grasping nothing but air. 'Jonah' was mobbed by his delighted team-mates and the Palace fans roared their approval, sensing, perhaps, that a big upset might be happening right before their eyes. It was also particularly noticeable how Forest tightened their marking of the powerful Welshman after this – especially at the following free kicks and corners!

Forest responded with a goal from Tinsley, their new forward from Middlesbrough, but they weren't level for long. A left-wing raid by John Whibley saw the youngster's slender frame bowled over, but he was on his feet straight away to flash across a centre for John Conner to restore Palace's lead with a neat header.

Palace scored again soon after the restart. Roy McCracken, their clever Northern Ireland

---

Crystal Palace 4
*Jones, Conner
Smith, Whibley*

Nottingham Forest 1
Tinsley

CRYSTAL PALACE v. NOTTINGHAM FOREST

Frank Lazenby's drawing captures the key action against Forest (above) and Everton (below, opposite).

international right half, was the initiator this time, deceiving Forest's defence with a free kick to John Conner who was standing close to the goal-line but a few yards wide of the goalpost. As Hardy moved across to close him down the wily Scotsman whipped the ball past him for skipper Ted Smith to sweep low into the net, almost, it seemed, out of Hardy's hands.

During the later exchanges, the ball burst after a particularly hefty clearance by Ernie Rhodes. Forest's Belton hit our crossbar but shortly afterwards John Whibley crushed any prospect of a Forest revival with a brilliant solo goal, dribbling his way from inside his own half, outpacing two opponents then, cutting in, drawing Hardy and lashing the ball past him for a glorious, emphatic goal.

Forest soon recovered from this opening day setback. Not only did they beat Palace by the odd goal in three in the return match a week later but they went on to comfortably win the Second Division championship. For the Palace, it was a marvellous victory and a wonderful day, but it didn't generate any lasting success among the more illustrious clubs playing at that level.

Crystal Palace: Alderson, Little, Rhodes, McCracken, Jones, Feebury, Bateman, Conner, E. Smith, Menlove, Whibley.
Nottingham Forest: Hardy, Bulling, Jones, Belton, F. Parker, Armstrong, Harrold, Spaven, R. Parker, Tinsley, Burton.

Everton v. Crystal Palace

Saturday 7 January 1922
Referee: unknown

FA Challenge Cup (Old) First Round
Attendance: 41,000

However brilliant Palace's opening day defeat of Nottingham Forest had been, there is no question that their 1921/22 season will always be remembered as the one in which they secured one of our finest ever results in the FA Cup.

Drawn to meet First Division Everton at Goodison Park in the old first round in early January, the Palace cannot have contemplated the tie with much enthusiasm or confidence, for, the Toffees were a pedigree club, their side was enjoying a good run and Palace had been beaten twice before at Goodison in cup-ties in pretty comprehensive fashion.

However, the Palace not only won at Everton, but they did so in riotous fashion - winning 6-0 against one of the leading clubs in the country. Just eighteen months out of the Southern League and here they were sinking a top-flight outfit without trace at their own distinguished headquarters – dreamland! The impact of the result upon the footballing fraternity cannot be properly appreciated today – to merely say it was a shock result is to mightily undervalue it. The contemporary press extolled us as a 'wonder team' and that is roughly the modern day equivalent of screaming headlines and excessive media hype. But it was, without question, a fabulous victory and is still argued by some to be the club's best result in any cup-tie.

How did they do it? It is clear that Palace were seldom on the defensive and actually had a couple of efforts disallowed for offside while another hit the crossbar, so that Jack Alderson was able to calmly peel and eat an orange that had been thrown to him from the crowd at one stage of the proceedings. John Whibley started the rout, when he headed in Ben Bateman's corner in only the fourth minute and when Croydon-born Bert Menlove's shot was deflected into the Everton net midway through the first half an upset began to look a real possibility, while Everton's original complacency was obviously wearing somewhat thin. The home side rallied in front of their fans, but they proved quite unable to break through Palace's sterling defence and it was left to them to round matters off with four more goals in the last quarter. John Conner converted a Whibley centre, then Menlove headed home another cross. Alf Wood made it five, and after Everton had missed a penalty, John Conner completed matters five minutes from time.

The *Athletic News* regarded the result as a 'sensation' – but then felt that the Palace were 'likely to make good progress in the competition'. Regrettably, if that august journal was correct in its former assessment, it was wrong in the latter. Palace were held 0-0 at The Nest by Millwall in the next round and went out 2-0 in the replay.

SIX TO NIL.

Everton 0

Crystal Palace 6
Whibley, Menlove (2)
Conner (2), Wood

Monday 2 April 1923
Referee: unknown

Football League, Second Division
Attendance: 20,000

The 1922/23 season provided little for Crystal Palace FC or its supporters to enthuse over and everyone at or connected with the club must have viewed the Easter programme of matches with dismay after a 4-1 defeat at Leeds the previous weekend. Our Good Friday and Easter Monday opponents were the champions-elect, Notts County, while their closest rivals for the title, FA Cup finalists West Ham, were at The Nest on Easter Saturday.

Fans' fears proved to be well founded: County won, albeit narrowly, at The Nest, but then West Ham administered a 5-1 hiding. That experience was humbling and the team must have appeared like lambs for the slaughter as the match against the exuberant Magpies at Meadow Lane approached.

Palace hung on in the first half and were pleased enough to reach the dressing room at half time with the scoresheet still blank and dignity at least somewhat restored, although County had hit our crossbar during the earlier proceedings. But then, early in the second period Palace slammed in three goals in an amazing eight-minute spell and went on from there to record a marvellous 4-0 victory.

The Palace forwards gave a gala performance during that blitz, showing pace and initiative as they overran a bemused County defence and neither they nor their fans could believe what was happening to them, with lowly Palace running riot. Billy Morgan cracked the first with a low drive, leading scorer George Whitworth blasted the second following a faulty clearance, then dapper little Bill Hand calmly lobbed the goalkeeper for the third. It was an incredible performance.

The outside left completed the rout towards the end when he converted Ben Bateman's perfect cross, but the fact that this 5ft 6in character did so with a header speaks volumes about the calibre of the Palace victory!

Bill Hand.

It is no exaggeration to say that Palace's Second Division survival hung upon this result. Before the game they were in a perilous position in the table because whilst they had a point or two on their fellow strugglers, all but one of them had games in hand. But this success triggered a new confidence that ensured further points from a praiseworthy draw at West Ham the following Saturday, another draw at home to South Shields and a big win over bottom club Wolves in the last home game.

Notts County, however, showed their pedigree and continued to dominate the division, finishing as champions with West Ham also promoted.

Notts County 0

Crystal Palace 4
Morgan, Whitworth
Hand (2)

Saturday 12 January 1924
Referee: Mr A.E. Caseley

FA Challenge Cup (Old) First Round
Attendance: 17,000

A contemporary caricature of Billy Morgan.

Palace's last season at The Nest was 1923/24 and they reserved their finest appearance of that term for an FA Cup tie. Tottenham, from the higher reaches of Division One were their illustrious visitors for an old first round encounter. The heavy pitch soon cut up and a typical Cup match ensued with plenty of excitement and drama for the fans so that it became clear that either a piece of sheer brilliance from the sophisticated north Londoners or some opportunist finishing by the Palace would settle the outcome.

The breakthrough came just after half an hour. Roy McCracken won the ball and slipped a pass to Albert Harry, who had a marvellous match. The little winger was away. He beat Spurs' skipper, England international wing-half Arthur Grimsdell, tore past the left back and cut in on goal before delivering a cross that was never more than a couple of feet off the ground. Several players went for it, but it was Palace's Billy Morgan, diving low among the flying boots and studs, who got to it and glided a perfect header past the Spurs goal-keeper for an inspirational goal.

Ten minutes after the break it was all over, Billy Morgan netting from close range after shots from Tom Hoddinott and Bill Hand had been blocked. Billy had been with the Palace since 1922 when he joined the club for £500 from Coventry. He was a useful Second Division goalscorer with the Palace without ever being prolific and, strangely, his two strikes which defeated Tottenham were his only ones in the FA Cup. He was to do little more for the Palace in his career, but he had done enough in the ninety minutes against the White Hart Lane outfit to earn himself a niche among the Palace heroes for many decades to come. It also earned him possibly the most curious nickname ever accorded to a Palace footballer – 'The Spurs Undertaker'. You don't have to be a parson to appreciate that one!

Regrettably, this win over Spurs was to be Palace's last FA Cup triumph at The Nest. We did go on to beat another top-flight club, Notts County, in the next round in a third replay after a titanic struggle in our longest ever Cup-tie, but that success was achieved at neutral Villa Park. But disappointment was to follow for when our old rivals from the Third Division, Swindon Town, came to The Nest for the next round at the end of February, they also came from behind to dismiss us from the competition with a brilliant recovery initiated by the great Harold Fleming.

Crystal Palace 2
Morgan (2)

Tottenham Hotspur 0

THE WEDNESDAY v. CRYSTAL PALACE

Saturday 27 December 1924
Referee: Mr J. Elbead

Football League, Second Division
Attendance: 10,000

Modern day Palace fans will be intrigued by the fact (although modern day footballers will be appalled!) that this was Palace's third Christmas time match in three days. Thus, the Palace, having secured a point at Portsmouth on Christmas morning and lost the Boxing Day return at The Nest, were now due at Hillsborough in Sheffield to meet The Wednesday.

It has been frequently recorded in Palace publications how the renowned Wednesday had provided the opposition for Palace's first-ever game at Selhurst Park on the opening day of this 1924/25 season – and beaten us 1-0. What is seldom told is how Palace gained precise and exact revenge in the return match by playing their best game of the entire season in deplorable conditions of pouring rain, driving wind and on a quagmire of a pitch. That omission is about to be rectified!

Palace were actually several places above Wednesday in the table at the time of this fixture. We had shrugged aside the disappointment of the Wednesday defeat and spent most of the autumn in the top third of the table, even reaching fifth place by 1 November after despatching Derby County 2-0. The match at Hillsborough saw Palace reproduce such form, possibly for the last time.

Palace's victory was secured by a performance of real character and professionalism. The side had been forced to weather (no pun intended!) enormous Wednesday pressure throughout the first half when the home side had the wind and rain behind them. But in what was only Palace's second attack they scored! Half time was imminent; Bill Hand was the instigator; George Whitworth was the executioner. Palace's tough little inside left broke clear down his flank before swinging over a cross for Whitworth to demonstrate real talent. He took possession, advanced, then as the 'keeper came out and the defenders began to close in, despatched a crisp, low shot which skidded along the sodden turf and entered the net just inside the foot of the post.

The second half was less one-sided and in this period the honours again went largely to our defence who showed tenacity and resilience in coping with the home attackers, but by the end Wednesday had realised that they had lost the day.

The sequel is, probably, all too well known to our fans. We immediately went back into decline, which proved impossible to arrest, ended up losing the last match of the season against fellow strugglers Oldham and were thus relegated from the Second Division so that nothing, absolutely nothing from that sequence could possibly vie for inclusion in this book. For George Whitworth however, matters evolved rather more positively. He had hit a hat-trick the previous season to defeat The Wednesday at The Nest. Allied to his crucial goal on this rainswept afternoon that accounts for the fact that he was eagerly sought by Wednesday and signed for them towards the end of this season.

George Whitworth.

The Wednesday 0	Crystal Palace 1
	Whitworth

Wednesday 23 September 1925
Referee: unknown

Football League, Third Division (South)
Attendance: 8,078

Percy Cherrett made an immediate
impact on his home debut.

PERCY—
CHERRETT
CRYSTAL
PALACE.

Palace's first season at Selhurst Park ended in bitter disappointment with relegation, but the opening of the second one was absolutely horrific! Palace lost all of their first five fixtures back in the old Third Division South with an adverse goal aggregate of 5-16. The team appeared to be in real trouble, but their manager-secretary Edmund Goodman had weathered previous Palace crises and he knew exactly the man the side both wanted and needed.

His name was Percy Cherrett. He was a strong, bustling centre forward with a proven goalscoring record and he was languishing in the Plymouth Argyle reserve team. He made his Palace debut at Brighton the previous Saturday (2-3), but now made his first appearance at Selhurst Park and Palace fans warmed to him immediately as he scored a couple of headed goals and tore Bristol City's defence to shreds as Palace secured their first victory of the season.

Few of those Palace fans who witnessed Percy's home debut are likely ever to have forgotten it: Palace's first win of the season was certainly emphatic, but actually it could easily have been considerably greater. The crossbar and posts were hit 'three or four times', the ball was twice cleared off the goal line by defenders and the City goalkeeper made what were described as 'many capital saves'! As the match progressed, it became evident that Cherrett and his colleagues were developing an understanding and growing in confidence all the time.

Cec Blakemore headed Palace into an early lead from an Albert Harry centre only for City to level, but Harry again provided the opportunity from which Cherrett restored the lead with his first goal in our colours, another header, then Blakemore increased the advantage in similar fashion before the interval. In the second half Cherrett's head added to our tally, but City responded near the end. However, perhaps the best move of the game came late in the contest. It took place on Palace's left and involved George Clarke, Blakemore and Cherrett and finished with a return pass from the new centre forward to Blakemore for him to complete his hat-trick with a powerful shot.

Percy himself scored a hat-trick of headers the following Saturday and in the end he finished the 1925/26 season with 26 strikes from 35 league outings. He formed an exciting goal-scoring partnership with Cec Blakemore, the pair thriving on the splendid service provided by wingers Albert Harry and the flame-haired George Clarke.

Crystal Palace 5
Blakemore (3)
Cherrett (2)

Bristol City 2
Sutherland
Paul

CRYSTAL PALACE v. PLYMOUTH ARGYLE

Saturday 28 November 1925
Referee: unknown

Football League, Third Division (South)
Attendance: 12,300

Table topping, free scoring Plymouth were always going to provide a major attraction at Selhurst Park against a Crystal Palace side which was still struggling to overcome the decline that had brought about relegation six months previously and saw us now in the lower reaches of the table, but interest was added to the occasion by the club's midweek appointment of a new manager Mr Alec Maley, formerly in charge of Hibernian. The fact was however, that Selhurst Park (and the wider neighbourhood) was covered by a sudden snowfall so that only a modest crowd of something over 12,000 hardy souls, including 'a strong contingent' from Plymouth, witnessed the spectacle that ensued.

The match was preceded by a minute's silence in memory of Queen Alexandra who had died earlier in the week, but what followed was amazing, breathtaking, wonderfully exciting, with the lead changing hands three times, the goal-tally mounting...and it provided a climactic finale. Fans who saw this encounter on the frozen surface – the line markings had been swept clear – have never forgotten it. They love to recount it to the club historian, but here is a brief resumé of the almost incredible action. Palace's new striker Percy Cherrett scored the first goal against the club from whom they had bought him after ten minutes from Roy McCracken's cross, but Plymouth showed their pedigree and were level three minutes later and ahead by the quarter-hour. They extended that lead before Cherrett rocked the crossbar with another header, but local boy Alf Hawkins brought Palace back to 3-2 with a similar effort that cannoned down and over the goal-line, only for The Pilgrims to gain a 4-2 advantage by the break.

But Palace rallied splendidly – a Hawkins drive from Albert Harry's centre revived hope then a tidal wave movement which involved every one of the Palace forward line enabled Tom Hoddinott, who was making his first appearance of the season, to bring Palace level midway through the second half. Tom then whacked a fifth for the Palace with a long drive with just five minutes to go, but, amidst intense excitement, the visitors levelled in the very last minute.

To this day, the match remains the highest scoring draw in which Palace have ever been engaged, at any of their home grounds or upon their travels and as such remains unique in the club's annals. Palace's form continued to improve, albeit slowly, and the team finished 1925/26 just below halfway in the table, but despite their fabulous goalscoring, Plymouth were pipped to promotion by Reading.

Plymouth (left) and Palace hold a minute's silence for the late Queen Alexandra before the game.

Crystal Palace 5
Cherrett, Hawkins (2)
Hoddinott (2)

Plymouth Argyle 5
Corcoran, Forbes
Cock (2), Black

Centre half Terry Coyle tangles with Chelsea's Turnbull.

One of the greatest occasions at Selhurst Park took place here at the end of January 1926 when Palace, from the wrong end of the old Third Division (South), entertained Chelsea, second placed in Division Two, in a fourth round FA Cup tie. The clash was really the first major event to be staged at our headquarters, which had only opened seventeen months previously, and certainly no match in the inaugural season had created anything approaching the interest that this one did.

Palace of course held an impressive FA Cup record from their pre-First World War days. The amazing 6-0 rout at Everton was still a recent memory while we had also beaten South Shields in the first-ever Cup tie to be staged at Selhurst Park in January 1925. Then, in the current season's tournament, we had rallied to force a replay with Northampton after trailing 0-3 at the County Ground and a 2-1 success had set up the derby game against Chelsea. However, no-one was expecting a crowd of over 40,000 for the tie and, frankly, it is impossible for modern day fans to imagine the scale of such an attendance at the ground in its open, undeveloped days. It is my understanding that the place was in ferment: heaving swathes of fans moved uncontrollably up, down and across the unterraced, unrestricted slopes and the passion was unbelievable.

George Clarke hit a Chelsea post for Palace early on to mark the side's intentions but Billy Callender was then called upon several times to save from eager Chelsea forwards. The first breakthrough came a little after half an hour when Palace had repulsed a Chelsea corner. Moving swiftly upfield, Cecil Blakemore spotted the penetrating run made by his fellow striker, new signing this season, Percy Cherrett, who was in rampant form, and fed the burly former Plymouth man the perfect pass which our centre forward accepted in spectacular style with a crashing drive that gave the Chelsea goalkeeper no chance. If Man of the Match awards had been awarded in 1926, Percy would have taken it home with him on that afternoon: he was quite superb and Chelsea had no answer to him.

After initial Chelsea pressure after the break, Palace went two up when Morden boy Alf Hawkins completed a four-man move that had involved Roy McCracken, Albert Harry and George Clarke, so that although Chelsea's inside right replied with some ten minutes remaining, Palace were able to hold on to register a fabulous victory – and the attendance record held for nearly forty years!

Crystal Palace 2
Cherrett
Hawkins

Chelsea 1
Thain

ENGLAND v. WALES

Home International Tournament
Referee: unknown   Attendance: 23,000

England star Billy Walker.

It may seem strange, inappropriate even, to some readers to discover a match being featured in this Crystal Palace book which has no apparent Crystal Palace connection to it. But the unarguable fact is that this match is the most important one in terms of status ever to have been staged at Selhurst Park and as such it simply cannot be ignored or omitted.

The Palace headquarters has hosted many representative fixtures including army international matches, amateur internationals, Olympic Games internationals and, in the mid 1970s, two England Under 23 games, but this match was a full England international and since it remains the only one to have been played at Selhurst Park, it qualifies in its own right for inclusion among the selection here.

English FA officials had always promised Crystal Palace FC that they would award a full international to Palace's new ground and now, almost exactly eighteen months after it opened, that promise was fulfilled with Wales as England's opponents and on St David's Day itself. Over 23,000 fans are known to have been present for the occasion and there are many amusing stories of how some of them managed to do so because this fixture took place on a Monday afternoon when most football supporters should have been at work or school! But this match brought some of British football's greatest stars to the Palace and Palace supporters weren't going to allow such a glittering event to pass them by, so ingenuity knew no bounds that day!

Unfortunately, most of them were to be disappointed by the outcome because the story of the match was one of traditional Welsh fervour overcoming the powerful looking English team. The 'home' men played well as individuals – some of them were very clever and entertaining – but they never gelled as a combination. The outcome was that Wales had the better of the match and fully deserved their 3-1 victory.

Admittedly, England did suffer by having to rearrange their forward line when Norman Bullock re-opened a previous injury to his forehead after a collision with one of the Welsh defenders. He had to leave the field for attention and although he returned with his head swathed in bandages, he had to play out on the right wing. Kelly of Sunderland took over down the middle in his stead while Unwin moved to inside right.

Whilst Bullock was off the field Wales took the lead, Vizard centred and Fowler scored a glorious goal with his head. English hopes were raised after the interval when Billy Walker headed an equaliser but it was not long before W. Davies put Wales ahead again, to the delight of the many Welshmen present, and then Fowler registered their third goal to ensure the victory they certainly deserved.

England 1
Walker

Wales 3
Fowler (2)
W. Davies

Wednesday 16 January 1929   FA Challenge Cup, Third Round Replay
Referee: unknown   Attendance: 16,200

It is always interesting to review the occasional huge win secured by clubs like Crystal Palace who are not, historically or generally, regarded as among the big goalscoring ones. This game must also register as a 'classic' because, to this day, it represents the club's (joint) biggest-ever victory from all the 239 played in the FA Cup competition (to the end of 2001/02).

The Selhurst Park setting for this replay was a decidedly wintry one because the pitch was covered with snow and it was only some twenty minutes before the 2.15p.m. kick-off that the referee deemed that the surface was fit to play upon, although by the start the snow had frozen hard to present thoroughly demanding conditions for the contest.

Two particular reasons can be advanced to explain Palace's big win. Firstly, the Palace side at this time was certainly one of their most effective in the old Third Division South, strong in defence, prolific up front. It came within a whisker of promotion at the end of this season (opponents Luton finished seventh), and no fewer than seven members of it featured in *Crystal Palace: 100 Greats* which was published in 2001. Secondly, Palace's tactics were clearly adjusted for the conditions. We used the sheer pace and immaculate control of our two wingers to full advantage and realising how difficult it would be for opposing defenders to turn on the icy surface, we deployed a largely long-ball game to real advantage.

Experienced fans are well aware that goal avalanches do not necessarily begin early in a game, but Palace quickly went ahead on this occasion and soon established a convincing victory margin; indeed, they were the winners in every way, long before the match had reached the halfway stage. Harry Havelock converted a tempting cross from George Clarke with his head after his initial shot had been beaten away, then, barely two minutes later, he collected an adroit pass from Jimmy Wilde and netted with a hard, low drive, which skimmed across the frosty surface. Wilde himself crashed in the third Palace goal before a quarter of the match had elapsed with a fulminating thirty-yard drive past a probably unsighted goalkeeper following a hastily and inaccurately cleared Palace corner.

Luton's response was repulsed by our defenders with little difficulty so that poor Billy Callender had little to do but try to keep himself warm while watching the Palace's irresistable forwards extend their lead. First, Havelock completed his hat-trick on the half hour, rounding off a neat move which had involved Bobby Greener and Lewis Griffiths with a fierce shot, then Griffiths himself despatched a fifth shortly before the interval from close range with the despondent Luton defence appealing in vain for offside.

Hubert Butler had the ball in the net early after the restart, but he was adjudged to have been offside after the referee had had a lengthy discussion on the matter with his linesman. However, Palace twice came again in the final quarter of the match with Butler heading home a cross from Albert Harry, then Jimmy Hamilton getting in on the act by heading past the hapless goalkeeper from a George Clarke corner near the end.

There was another high-scoring Selhurst Park replay in the fourth round – again following an initial 0-0 scoreline – when Palace beat Millwall 5-3. This time Hubert Butler claimed a hat-trick, but the club's furthest progress in the FA Cup between the wars came to a shuddering halt on another snowy surface, up at Huddersfield (2-5) in the fifth round.

Crystal Palace 7   **Luton Town 0**
Havelock (3) Wilde
Griffiths, Butler, Hamilton

CRYSTAL PALACE v. LUTON TOWN

Harry Havelock scored a hat-trick in Palace's biggest ever victory ...

... and here's the first of them! The left-wing cross eludes the Luton defender for Harry to put Palace in front with a header.

Crystal Palace: Callender, Wetherby, Charlton, Hamilton, Wilde, Greener, Harry, Havelock, Griffiths, Butler, Clarke.
Luton Town: Abbot, Graham, Harris, Black, Clark, Fraser, Daley, Yardley, Rennie, Woods, Dennis.

CRYSTAL PALACE v. NORWICH CITY

Saturday 14 September 1929
Referee: Mr E. Pinckaton

Football League, Third Division (South)
Attendance: 14,056

Peter Simpson.

This match was Peter Simpson's senior debut for Crystal Palace and remains unique in the club's annals as the only occasion upon which a Palace player has netted a hat-trick in his first Football League appearance. Peter had signed for Palace in the summer of 1929 from Kettering Town and he must rate as one of the best signings the club has ever made, while his debut crystallised his ability to score goals and emphasises for us just what a brilliant marksman he was.

Despite finishing as runners-up in Division Three South the previous summer, Palace's 1929/30 season had not started well, for they had drawn and lost their opening two home games. Despite early Palace pressure, Norwich took the lead on that warm, sunlit afternoon with just ten minutes gone, Slicer's header proving too much for Billy Callender. Palace's response was furious and intense, so much so that their equaliser was both long overdue and thoroughly deserved when Peter Simpson netted with a hard, low volley from an Albert Harry cross. Norwich endured what a local correspondent described as a 'severe bombardment' after this, but they managed to hold out to reach the break still on terms.

Six minutes after the interval, Palace gained the lead and this time Peter was indebted to his other winger, George Clarke, who finished a dazzling run with a tempting, drifting cross which Peter met with a diving header for a spectacular, close-range strike. Palace were now determined to put the outcome beyond Norwich and were successful in doing so when Peter's header from a right-wing centre was mishandled by the goalkeeper and flew high into the net.

Norwich were not outplayed however and were able to reduce the arrears near the end when another headed goal, this time following a free kick, beat the unsighted Billy Callender. Thus encouraged, The Canaries pressed hard for a point in the finale, but Palace's defence demonstrated poise and control in ensuring that we gained the full reward for our efforts that afternoon.

Interestingly, Palace and Norwich took a point apiece from the Carrow Road return in January when Peter Simpson netted Palace's second, the equaliser, but the clubs finished the season level on points, a disappointing seven and eight places adrift of promoted Plymouth Argyle.

Crystal Palace 3
Simpson (3)

Norwich City 2
Slicer
Thompson

CRYSTAL PALACE v. EXETER CITY

Saturday 4 October 1930
Referee: Mr C.N. Wood

Football League, Third Division (South)
Attendance: 12,805

Albert Harry contributed to each one of Peter Simpson's goals.

Palace's previous three home games this season had already produced a couple of big victories with an aggregate scoreline of 12-2 and Peter Simpson had notched hat-tricks on both occasions. However, in this match Peter surpassed all goalscoring feats by his predecessors at the club and set a record which none of his successors having ever been able to equal by finding the target six times – and consecutively too!

In fact, Simpson's magnificent achievement came about from a sublime display of quality ball control and fierce, accurate shooting, sometimes from difficult angles, demonstrating for all to see just how lethal a marksman he was when his confidence was high – it was acknowledged that the Grecians' goalkeeper had little or no chance with any of Peter's goals. Apart from the opener, Peter had to forage hard for the other strikes, either by beating defenders with pace and close, neat footwork, or by working himself into a position from which he could deliver a telling shot. And, had two other Palace forwards not strayed into offside positions, Peter would have had another goal from a free kick that he drove into the net from just outside the penalty area!

It may also be an indication of Peter's awesome display that none of the local press reporters were able to record many of his goals in detail. However, it can be confidently related that Peter's first effort was a header from Albert Harry's accurate cross and indeed all seven Palace goals involved the little winger whose own control of the slippery ball was simply masterly. The tally had reached 3-1 by the interval but Exeter replied again quickly after the break when a left-wing centre deflected into our net off Bobby Greener. Taking further heart from this the visitors sought to get on terms, but Simpson's finishing was so deadly that the Palace tally simply mounted regularly and when he hit his sixth goal, several of the Exeter players congratulated him with a handshake while the Palace crowd roared its approval.

There was still time for Hubert Butler to add one final goal, when, once more, Albert Harry was the provider. This time though he deceived his immediate opponents by taking the ball inside them rather than down the flank, then pushing it forward to the Palace striker.

Another key member of the victorious Palace side was goalkeeper Billy Callender because Exeter were by no means a poor team and we were forced to defend, sometimes quite desperately, with Billy making several wonderful saves from the plucky visiting forwards.

Crystal Palace 7
Simpson 6
Butler

Exeter City 2
Varco
Greener (og)

Friday 26 December 1930
Referee: Mr W.E. Russell

Football League, Third Division (South)
Attendance: 15,853

Although it is clearly understood by present day supporters that, generally speaking, football between the two world wars was less defensively organised or orientated than the modern game and that goalscoring feats were thus more frequent, this particular match remains one of the Palace occasions from that period to which the fans of those times invariably point when discussion turns to such matters. One reason for this must be the manner in which their favourites avenged the 8-2 trouncing at Griffin Park the previous day in such comprehensive terms. The turning of despair into elation so quickly seems to have etched an indelible mark upon the psyche of Palace fans who saw one or both of the games.

Selhurst's pitch was wet and slippery and Palace inevitably made some adjustments to the line-up, skipper Stan Charlton returning after an eight-week lay-off for injury, while Billy Turner was also restored after missing the Christmas Day clash for reasons that are unclear. Interestingly too, Brentford included two former Palace stars, Cec Blakemore and Harold Salt.

Palace were ahead so quickly that plenty of fans didn't see the first goal – and some missed the second one too! Palace kicked off, whereupon Simpson, Harry and Butler set up George Clarke who cut in and drove the ball like an arrow into the Brentford net. It was suggested that this goal was scored within thirty seconds of the kick-off, and a minute later Palace were two goals up! Peter Simpson won a tackle, strode forward and with a shot that deflected off a Bees defender made it 2-0! Jimmy Wilde netted a third direct from a free kick just after half an hour to emphasise our superiority and eventually Brentford fashioned a headed reply just before the break but Palace went on to secure another brace in the second half.

Bobby Greener delivered a free kick for the unmarked Albert Harry to crack Palace's fourth goal with a right-footed drive and George Clarke ended the rampage in exciting style, beating an opponent then, turning the advantage rule to full account, regaining his feet after being felled and firing home from close range.

Curiously, Brentford's Jack Lane, who had scored a hat-trick in the Christmas morning game, was extremely quiet on this afternoon, but the legacy of his exploits against us remained for Palace signed him four weeks later.

Palace and Brentford finished the season second and third respectively in the Division Three South table, a single point separating them, but well adrift of the champions Notts County.

The line-up page in the programme for Palace's Boxing Day clash with Brentford.

CRYSTAL PALACE
COLOURS—CARDINAL and BLUE

Right · · · · · · Left

1
Callender

2   3
Crilly   Barrie

4   5   6
Rivers   Wilde   Greener

7   8   9   10   11
Harry   Turner   Simpson   Butler   Clarke

Referee : W. E. RUSSELL
(Swindon)
KICK-OFF 2.30 p.m.

Linesmen :
E. LOVICK, Red Cross Flag
D. CORTIS, Blue Cross Flag

Payne   Blakemore   Lane, (W.)   Lane, (J.)   Foster
12   13   14   15   16

Salt   Bain   Davies
17   18   19

Adamson   Stevenson
20   21

Fox
22

Left · · · · · · Right

BRENTFORD
COLOURS—RED & WHITE

Crystal Palace 5
Clarke (2), Simpson
Wilde, Harry

Brentford 1
W. Lane

CRYSTAL PALACE v. MILLWALL

Saturday 2 November 1935
Referee: Mr E.R. Westwood

Football League, Third Division (South)
Attendance: 19,239

No. 20, Vol. XXXI.   Saturday, Nov. 2nd, 1935.   Two Pence

CRYSTAL PALACE F.C.
SELHURST PARK
S.E.25

Official Programme
SEASON
1935-36

PALACE

MILLWALL

ENGLISH LEAGUE MATCH   Kick-off 2.55 p.m.

The front cover of the match programme.

It is a rare thing for two newcomers to any side to both score on their debut on the same day: for them to do so alongside a hat-trick from an ace striker and in a local derby makes that occasion remarkable.

Palace were lying fourth in the table when Millwall came to Selhurst Park on the first Saturday in November 1935. We were just two points adrift of the leaders, Reading, and certainly felt that there was every possibility that we could make up the lee-way and still have something to spare by season's end. To aid the cause Palace manager, former England international Tom Bromilow, had made three recent signings to strengthen the team: full-back Bert Thorpe had arrived from Norwich, versatile forward Bob Birtley signed from Coventry and strong, bustling centre forward Jack Blackman moved across London from Queens Park Rangers; they were all making their first Palace appearances this afternoon. Each played soundly and contributed to Palace's emphatic success with the two front men both on target, Birtley heading an early, opening goal from a cross by Bob Bigg to set the Palace on their way, and Blackman rounded matters off with a classic goal, which probably indicates a powerfully struck spectacular effort, for these were Jack's trademark.

However, despite the two excellent goalscoring debuts, Palace's man of the match was undoubtedly our brilliant striker Albert Dawes who not only scored a quality hat-trick - two were headers; the other a crashing left foot drive - but also plied the square pass from which Blackman scored his goal, and demonstrated fine 'ball control and general deportment' which I think we can take to mean vision, passing, direction – and of course extraordinary shooting prowess.

But, now, this is Crystal Palace FC that we are writing and reading about! Therefore it would be something of a mistake to luxuriate for long over this victory, inspiring though it undoubt-edly was. Palace lost the next game 1-8 at eventual champions Coventry – and the following three as well! – and finished the season sixth in their section. Only Coventry scored more goals than their 96, but Albert Dawes was the top scorer there with 38 goals from 41 appearances and was only beaten by one goal and one player in the entire Football League.

Of the three newcomers, Jack Blackman was certainly the best signing. He went on to play 107 League and Cup games for Palace before the Second World War and scored 55 goals. Bob Birtley also remained with the club until the end of 1938/39, but his career at Selhurst Park was a fading one. He played 69 senior games for Palace, scoring 16 goals. Bert Thorpe never settled at the Palace. He played just two more games for the side and left at the end of the season.

Crystal Palace 5   Millwall 0
Birtley, A. Dawes (3)
Blackman

CRYSTAL PALACE v. LIVERPOOL

Saturday 8 January 1938
Referee: Mr S. Hadley

FA Challenge Cup, Third Round
Attendance: 33,000

Some football matches gain their significance in their own right, some from the context in which they have been scheduled. Occasionally, however, a game increases in consequence from subsequent events – and that is the case with this one.

Without the modern day rivalry between Palace and Liverpool which has seen us embarrass the Reds in several high profile matches – all of them to be found and gloated over later in this book! – this 0-0 draw on a pre-war early January afternoon would surely have remained simply a statistic in the Palace records. But Liverpool's first visit to Selhurst Park and its outcome are now clearly to be seen as part of the dramatic sequence of clashes between the clubs and there is historic interest in the fact that Matt Busby was included in their line-up.

Palace's first appearance at the third round stage of the FA Cup for four years was eagerly anticipated by our fans, particularly given the top flight status of the opposition, but at the club itself there was real anxiety because a spate of injuries had ruled out our first choice pair of full backs, Fred Dawes and Ted Owens; recently signed Fred Gregory was 'cup-tied' and Sam Booth could only resume training a day or two before the game. However, our makeshift defence coped splendidly with the demands imposed by the First Division side and of course our greatest strength lay in the half-back line of Les Lievesley, George Walker and Nick Collins which many fans who saw them play together regard as the best the club had in those positions for many decades.

Consequently, a strangely muted Liverpool seldom threatened...but Palace's best chance, a low drive from winger Johnny Horton late in the proceedings, was deflected to safety off the unwitting centre half after it had beaten the goalkeeper.

And so to an Anfield replay four days later when Liverpool missed a first-half penalty for handball, Palace snatched the lead through Ernie Waldron and Liverpool replied ten minutes later with a goal which every Palace player and their little knot of fans were convinced had been handled into the net. In extra time Nick Collins, who had been quite magnificent throughout the tie, had the misfortune to concede an own goal and Joe Fagan converted a late penalty.

However, controversy is never far from Palace-Liverpool encounters. 'Pool printed disparaging comments in their replay programme to which Palace understandably took exception. They were censured by the FA and ordered to apologise, but Palace fans of the late 1930s probably felt that a certain Villa Park outcome some fifty years later settled the dispute rather more adequately!

Palace defenders George Walker (left) and Sam Booth (right) watch Geoff Turton rise for this header.

Crystal Palace 0   **Liverpool 0**

CRYSTAL PALACE v. CLAPTON ORIENT

Saturday 19 October 1940
Referee: unknown

Wartime South Regional League
Attendance: 1,500

Generally speaking, football matches during the Second World War failed to attract much interest, for obvious reasons – most people had more important matters to concern them. But those who could devote themselves to the game at that time found it quite compelling as well as an excellent diversion, whilst an historical perspective often provides modern readers with plenty of curiosities.

These certainly began early on this autumn Saturday afternoon when, Clapton Orient having arrived a player short, Palace's Fred Gregory was invited to 'guest' for them! Fred duly obliged – and when Orient were awarded a penalty for handball, the Palace crowd advised the visitors to allow Fred to take it, for few men before or since have been able to hit a dead ball as powerfully as Fred could do. They did and he scored!

However, the Palace were by far the stronger side on this particular afternoon and they were already three goals to the good at that point, Albert Dawes having scored two quick goals at the start and Bert Robson converting a pass from the amateur inside forward E.A. Waite. After half time, Jack Blackman soon added to the lead from a cross from Robson and when Orient lost their centre forward through injury the visitors could only defend as best they were able to keep the score to reasonable proportions. With something less than a quarter of an hour remaining, Bert Robson netted a fifth for Palace. A minute later Charlie Fletcher – a fringe player with us some dozen years before – replied with a fearsome thirty yarder, but Palace had the last word with a cleverly worked goal which was ulti-

Fred Gregory.

mately scored by Bert Robson, completing his hat-trick after a neat passing bout with Jack Blackman.

Other items of interest from this afternoon were the appearance of brothers Fred and Albert Dawes together in the Palace side and of Fred and Mark Gregory in opposition to each other.

Perhaps the most curious feature for present day readers was the way in which this wartime league operated, for it was extremely complicated to say the least and, mercifully, quite unique. Clubs were free to play as many or as few fixtures as they chose to arrange and league positions were decided purely on goal average. Hence, it is a great (if rather unexpected!) joy to record that the Palace, rarely among the country's best goalscoring clubs, headed the table in front of West Ham (whom we did not meet) and Arsenal (with whom Palace drew both times, 2-2 at Highbury and 3-3 at Selhurst Park).

Crystal Palace 6
A. Dawes (2), Robson (3)
Blackman

Clapton Orient 2
F. Gregory (pen)
Fletcher

CRYSTAL PALACE v. BRIGHTON & HOVE ALBION

Saturday 11 February 1950
Referee: Mr F.S. Fiander

Football League, Third Division (South)
Attendance: 14,261

Ronnie Rooke.

Palace's 1949/50 season could be said by the cynics to be damned with faint praise when it is described as their best post-war term in Division Three South, but that itself would be to do insufficient justice to a welcome surge in Palace's fortunes during an extremely disappointing period in the annals of our club.

Architect of Palace's all too brief revival in 1949/50 was player-manager Ronnie Rooke, of the distinctive rugged features, the Latin nose, thunderous shot and rolling gait. In the Palace reserve sides of the mid 1930s Rooke's scoring record was quite remarkable with 160 goals in three and a half seasons, but he was never able to reproduce such form in our first team. He moved to Fulham in October 1936 and played there with great success, then signed for Arsenal in 1946 and helped them to the 1948 League Championship as the League's top scorer with 33 strikes.

Ronnie returned to the Palace as player-manager in the summer of 1949 and Palace rose from bottom in 1948/49 to seventh in 1949/50 as he hit 21 League goals and helped to draw some big crowds to Selhurst Park to see 'The Rooke Regiment'.

Certainly among the most memorable Palace displays in that season was the 6-0 rout of visiting Brighton on the second Saturday of February in which Ronnie put Palace ahead early with a classic, long-range, low drive from a pass by Ted Harding. A little after half an hour, Fred Kurz controlled a deflected effort by young winger Ray Howells and crashed the ball into the net. Brighton attempted a revival after the break but outside right Billy Blackshaw broke clear and centred for Rooke to score probably his best senior goal for the Palace. With his back to goal he controlled the cross, spun on his heel then lobbed the ball over the goalkeeper and into the net. For Palace it was a sublime goal; for Brighton it spelt an end to their hopes and they realised that a rearguard action was now required to limit further damage.

Ray Howells raced away and finished well; Rooke himself turned provider for another former Arsenal man, Charlie Chase, to volley past Baldwin, and Rooke completed his hat-trick from a Howells centre with nearly a quarter of an hour still to go.

Regrettably however, the following season was quite dreadful and Ronnie was relieved of his post at the end of November so that in retrospect his managerial contribution to the fortunes of Crystal Palace can only be said to have been calamitous.

Crystal Palace 6
Rooke (3), Kurz
Howells, Chase

Brighton & Hove Albion 0

SWINDON TOWN v. CRYSTAL PALACE

Saturday 1 November 1952
Referee: Mr R.E. Tarratt

Football League, Third Division (South)
Attendance: 9,106

The occasions upon which Crystal Palace have managed to score six goals away from home in fully competitive matches are rare ones. Certainly, this one stood out for fans of the 1950s because it was so completely unexpected!

At the time we travelled to Swindon's undeveloped County Ground, Palace were a bottom six side in the old Third Division South. They'd been involved in high-scoring games already this season but, without exception, we had been on the receiving end of them. Confidence among the players, or the coachload of fans who travelled down to Wiltshire, was consequently low – except that a certain swarthy little Scouser named 'Cam' Burgess had begun scoring goals again. This tough, canny, experienced inside or centre forward had arrived at the Palace from Chester some fourteen months before in the wake and on the recommendation of Les Devonshire and scored an astonishing 21 League goals from just 22 outings in 1951/52. But he hadn't found the target at all in his first seven games of 1952/53. Then there arrived at Selhurst Park a fast, direct, raiding winger in the person of Les Fell, along with intelligent, resourceful wing-half Colin Grimshaw and Burgess bloomed once more for the Palace from their service.

His chief accomplice in the demolition of Swindon was the youthful, blossoming Johnny Rainford, but Palace's frailties were all too apparent in the first half when we were twice in arrears and behind at half time, although a Rainford header from a Devonshire corner, then an early reply after the restart from Burgess each put us on terms.

Our best goal of the afternoon was the one that put us ahead for the first time, just three minutes later. Burgess took a pass from Devonshire, put his foot on the ball, calmly took stock, pushed it forward for Bob Thomas, and Rainford netted from the centre forward's pass. Swindon levelled at 3-3 on the hour, but Palace were now unstoppable: Rainford converted a Fell cross with his head for 4-3, a Burgess cracker from distance found the target, then, with five minutes left, a Rainford dummy allowed a pass from Devonshire to wrong foot the home defence and run on to Burgess, whose half-hit shot deceived the goalkeeper and registered his third hat-trick in four games, all within just twenty-two days!

JOHNNIE RAINFORD

Johnnie Rainford.

Swindon Town 3
Owen (2)
Bain

Crystal Palace 6
Rainford (3)
Burgess (3)

Friday 1 May 1953
Referee: Mr F.C. Williams

Football League, Third Division (South)
Attendance: 5,629

Bob Thomas.

Despite the improvement in Palace's fortunes typified by the success that is chronicled on the previous page, these were tough times in which to support the club. Until another Burgess hat-trick helped to defeat second-placed Northampton at Selhurst Park on a snow-covered pitch in mid-February there was little reason to think the side could avoid a third application for re-election to the League in five years at the end of the term.

But matters did improve and – despite Burgess' absence from the side – they did so to such an extent that by the end of the season Palace feared nobody and were a match for anyone, particularly on their own ground. By now their chief goalscorers were Bill Simpson and Bob Thomas who both relished the service provided by our wingers, Les Fell, Les Devonshire and the emerging starlet Ronnie Downs.

Accordingly, Palace edged their way up the Third Division South table and became quite unrecognisable from the side that had been so badly embarrassed in League and Cup games earlier on. But the real test of the extent of our improvement came in the final fixture, played on the eve of the FA Cup Final, when the champions of the Southern Section, Bristol Rovers, came to Selhurst Park to conclude the season.

The conditions for this match were appalling: after twenty-four hours of unremitting rainfall, the pitch was a sea of mud. There was very little grass on pitches by the end of the term in those days and it looked, and played, like a quagmire. The rain continued to fall in torrents throughout the game so that at times it was barely possible to see across the full width of the pitch! The anticipated big crowd was reduced to just the hardiest and most loyal supporters who clustered in the main stand and its old enclosure – although a few youthful madcaps insisted on taking up their usual positions on the terraces behind the goal!

Palace gained the lead midway through the first half when 'Archie' Andrews lifted the already sodden ball into the visitors' goalmouth where Bob Thomas beat former Palace goalkeeper (and captain for the day) Bob Anderson, with a clever, twisting header, and despite fierce pressure from Rovers throughout the second half Palace were resolute and unyielding and, eventually, the winners of an extraordinary, yet, in its context, magnificently contested game.

Crystal Palace 1
R. Thomas

Bristol Rovers 0

CRYSTAL PALACE v. BRENTFORD

Wednesday 12 December 1956   FA Challenge Cup, Second Round Replay
Referee: Mr R.H. Windle   Attendance: 23,137

Peter Berry was prominent in Palace's exciting FA Cup replay victory over Brentford.

By the mid 1950s Palace were still a modest Third Division outfit but they had acquired the hugely embarrassing habit of going out of the FA Cup in its early stages, often in ignominious circumstances. Thus a 1956 first round victory over Walthamstow Avenue was greeted with relief as well as pleasure and this was followed by a 1-1 draw at Brentford, one of the strongest sides in the Third Division.

The Selhurst Park replay produced a crowd that was among our post-war best at that time, plus a Palace victory after 123 thrill-packed minutes, which live in the memory to this day. The occasion was highlighted by a hat-trick from Barry Pierce – a protégé of Palace's manager of the period, Cyril Spiers – his only one for our club and Palace's first in the FA Cup for over a quarter of a century.

Brentford grabbed an early lead when their own striker, Jimmy Towers converted a Ron Peplow cross, but Palace were on terms midway through the first half when Pierce headed home a centre from Peter Berry, but the Bees were ahead again twelve minutes later when Towers became the supplier for George Francis. Palace believed this to have been scored from an offside position and were appealing for a decision when the ball beat Ray Potter in the Palace goal, and, having been previously denied a penalty for an apparent handball, were somewhat aggrieved at the situation. But three minutes before half time, Palace were deservedly level again. A lovely passing bout involving Bernard Harrison twice, Peter Berry and Jim Belcher saw a cross from Palace's right met by Pierce who hooked the ball over Cakebread, only for the 'keeper to make a remarkable backward somersault and catch the ball as he fell. But he lost it as he dropped onto the ground and Pierce, following up, sent Palace fans into ecstasies as he tapped the ball over the line from close range.

The second half may have been goal-less, but the action was thrilling and intense as Ray Potter and his Brentford counterpart brought off magnificent and athletic saves. In extra time Brentford pressed strongly and drew two more fine saves from Potter early in those proceedings when he denied the ever-dangerous Towers, but the contest was won and lost in the 102nd minute. Bernard Harrison collected a loose ball in the middle of the park and streaked away down his flank. He beat Croydon-born Ian Dargie and centred to where Barry Pierce was waiting unmarked to deliver a perfect, fierce, downward header into the bottom corner of the net for a classic finale, which was deserving of a bigger stage.

Crystal Palace 3   **Brentford 2**   **(after extra time)**
Pierce (3)   *Towers*
        Francis

CRYSTAL PALACE v. CREWE ALEXANDRA

Saturday 23 August 1958
Referee: Mr E.S. Oxley

Football League, Fourth Division
Attendance: 13,551

Despite the best efforts of manager Cyril Spiers, Crystal Palace found themselves among the initial members of the new national Fourth Division of the Football League at the end of the 1957/58 season. Inevitably, that meant a new manager and the avuncular Spiers was replaced by tough disciplinarian George Smith, who vowed before his first season in charge got under way that if he did not gain promotion for the club within two years, he would resign. Regrettably, and despite the excellent opening match at this level being reviewed here, all too soon it became apparent that any such success would not be gained at the first attempt.

Modern day readers should also be aware that whilst Palace's appearance in the new Football League basement was disappointing, there was certainly a high aspiration (if, perhaps, this was naively based) to take advantage of the new circumstances and to gain promotion and momentum from them. Equally, there was plenty of interest too because the club and its fans were meeting new opponents, visiting new grounds and renewing old rivalries. Thus, among the nine clubs we met for the first time under Football League auspices in 1958/59 were Crewe Alexandra.

It was Crewe's first ever visit to Selhurst Park and they gave most of the crowd a blast of reality within two minutes of the proceedings getting under way because the Railwaymen opened the scoring. Thankfully however, from that point, apart from a few brief, isolated periods, the Palace dominated and were able to romp to a 6-2 win. The game became a personal triumph for Palace centre forward Mike Deakin who was making his first senior appearance for nine months after a major cartilage operation and he notched up a superb first-half hat-trick in considerably less than half an hour. And there was another hat-trick this afternoon for Palace fans to enjoy. It was provided by Johnny Byrne, still only nineteen years old but already beginning to demonstrate the prowess that would lead him to stardom and help lift Crystal Palace out of the Fourth Division. Unfortunately though, despite such a rampant start, Palace seldom threatened to take one of the four promotion places that are offered from the bottom division and they finished seventh, so that it was not until two years later, with the arrival of Arthur Rowe, that they were able to climb out of the League graveyard.

Mike Deakin is pictured second from the right in the back row of this Palace team photograph of 1957/58.

Crystal Palace 6
Deakin (3)
Byrne (3)

Crewe Alexandra 2
Pearson (2)

CRYSTAL PALACE v. BARROW

Saturday 10 October 1959
Referee: Mr J. Finney

Football League, Fourth Division
Attendance: 9,566

Roy Summersby, who scored four times in Palace's record win over Barrow.

As the previous article has shown, Palace weren't able to sustain a realistic challenge for promotion in either of their first two seasons in the new Football League basement division. Thus the club's appeal to its followers at that time was largely low key and none of the nine and a half thousand faithful who came to Selhurst Park for Barrow's visit on 10 October 1959 could possibly have had an inkling that they might be about to witness Palace's biggest-ever victory in league or major cup matches.

Manager George Smith was perhaps unfortunate that potentially his best signing of that summer, the talented Dave Sexton, formerly of West Ham and Brighton, was prevented from appearing in little more than half the games this season due to injury. However, even with Dave in the side they had lost the four matches prior to the visit of the Holker Street men and were lying tenth in the Fourth Division table.

The match itself was obviously a personal triumph for Palace forward Roy Summersby, who notched four of their goals – the first time since the war that a Palace man had netted more than three goals in a game. The scoring was opened by left winger Ray Colfar, and that 1958 signing from Sutton United was a clever, wily character whose displays gained the respect of Palace fans for an often forgotten former player at the club.

Ray started Palace on the way to this huge victory midway through the first half with a twenty yard drive from a sweeping, incisive long pass from Dave Sexton, and it became apparent a quarter of an hour later that Barrow could be in for a torrid afternoon when Palace's Eire star, right-winger Johnny Gavin netted direct from a corner. Summersby then collected his first two goals within a couple of minutes of each other as half time approached and when Ray Colfar hit his second early in the second half, it was clear to all that Barrow's defences had been breached and were on the point of being over-run. After the hour, Summersby scored two more goals in quick succession, the first going in off a post, the second from a penalty for handball.

Johnny Byrne had an effort disallowed before he converted an unselfish pass from Colfar and then rounded matters off in the penultimate minute with a low drive past the dispirited goalkeeper.

Finally, a classic Palace curiosity – four days later Palace played a floodlit friendly against a Caribbean XI and won 11-1, only to contrive to lose at Aldershot the following Saturday!

Crystal Palace 9
*Colfar (2), Gavin
Summersby (4, inc pen), Byrne (2)*

Barrow 0

CRYSTAL PALACE v. ACCRINGTON STANLEY

Saturday 20 August 1960
Referee: Mr K.R. Tuck

Football League, Fourth Division
Attendance: 15,653

Palace began the 1960/61 season with a disappointing record from their previous two campaigns in the recently formed national Fourth Division, in which Palace had finished seventh and eighth respectively, but with a new manager in Arthur Rowe, several new signings and accordingly renewed hope in the hearts of everyone connected with the club.

The Palace board had sought Rowe's services in 1958 but he had not been well enough to accept full responsibility then. But in April 1960 he agreed to take up the challenge – and how thankful all Crystal Palace fans are that he did so, for he was to take Palace to promotion for the first time in forty years with attractive, polished play, thereby setting the club on the road to glory.

Rowe's most strategic signing in the summer months was that of Ron Heckman, a blond, fast-raiding winger from Millwall who was well known to London soccer fans. Palace's 110 league goals in 1960/61 were due in no small part to the efforts of this man, whose 14 strikes from 42 appearances set up a post-war scoring record for a winger at the Palace (which only Peter Taylor has equalled) and those of Johnny Gavin at outside right who had been with Mr Rowe at Tottenham.

The opening fixture was against opponents who were making their first – and indeed only – appearance at Selhurst Park, Accrington Stanley, who were relegated from the Third Division at the end of 1959/60 and soon to pass into oblivion. With Palace's augmented line-up we romped to a 3-1 lead in eight minutes. By the break it was 5-2 and the second half became a rout as Palace hit four more without reply. Johnny Byrne notched four goals himself, including the first one of the entire Football League season after just fifty seconds, while Alan Woan secured a hat-trick and Ron Heckman got a brace to mark an impressive debut.

This was just the sort of start to the season that Palace wanted, demonstrating in the best possible manner that the new, slick, 'push and run' style inspired by Mr Rowe was not just glorious to watch but also wonderfully effective.

Jim Mercer celebrated Palace's 9-2 victory over Accrington in unique fashion!

Crystal Palace 9
*Byrne (4), Woan (3)
Heckman (2)*

Accrington Stanley 2
*Hudson
Swindells*

YORK CITY v. CRYSTAL PALACE

Saturday 10 December 1960
Referee: Mr F.V. Stringer

Football League, Fourth Division
Attendance: 6,538

George Petchey.

Clever and attractive as Arthur Rowe's Palace side usually was, it became necessary early in the 1960/61 season to augment it, and it could certainly be argued that Mr Rowe's most astute signing of the promotion campaign was that of his former Tottenham centre-forward, Dennis Uphill, early in October. Burly, strong and ungainly, Dennis was needed to ensure that the talents of Johnny Byrne and Roy Summersby were given a free rein and not thwarted by the heavy treatment that was beginning to be meted out to them by some of the more unscrupulous Fourth Division defenders. Rugged Dennis took a lot of the buffeting, but gained little praise for his role, yet he was a deft, intelligent footballer so that it certainly should not be thought that he was simply a battering-ram at the centre of our forward line.

Thus, by early December, Palace headed the table by a point from Peterborough, but the fixtures on the second Saturday of that month required them to travel to York City, who were the only club in the section to have remained unbeaten at home, while Posh appeared (mistakenly, it turned out) to be all set for a win at Barrow. But Palace played perhaps their best away game of the campaign to claim victory at Bootham Crescent to secure a clear points lead at the top of the table.

York were well placed, right on the shoulders of the leading outfits and certainly had aspirations of their own. They were tough, strong opponents and the game was dour and tense with the early exchanges particularly littered with fouls as the battle for supremacy took hold, but ultimately Palace's skills won the match, with both their goals being absolute gems. The opener stemmed from a corner gained by Alf Noakes. Ron Heckman played a short one to Johnny Byrne who involved Noakes again, whose square pass to George Petchey was chipped home in quite delightful fashion.

Roy Summersby played as a man inspired throughout the second half but, after York had hit our crossbar, Palace killed off the Minstermen's challenge with a quarter of an hour left. Byrne sent Dennis Uphill away and the big man bustled his way to the by-line before crossing for Ron Heckman to crack home the conclusive second strike.

Palace finished the season as runners-up to gain promotion behind Peterborough, but York ended the season in fifth place and had to wait until 1965 before they reached the Third Division.

York City 0	Crystal Palace 2
	Petchey
	Heckman

TORQUAY UNITED v. CRYSTAL PALACE

Saturday 19 August 1961
Referee: Mr P.G. Boardwood

Football League, Third Division
Attendance: 10,319

Palace paraded three new players when they opened their first season in the Third Division in August 1961. Full back Roy Little, who had joined Palace from Brighton, had appeared in the 1955 and 1956 FA Cup finals with Manchester City; Ronnie Allen the famous West Bromwich Albion and England centre forward or winger had been a contemporary of Palace assistant manager Dick Graham at The Hawthorns, while Andy Smillie, a talented little fellow from West Ham, based his game upon that of the brilliant Hungarian master Ferenc Puskas and finished this season as Palace's top League goalscorer with 16 goals.

Palace's campaign started well. Continuing to play the stylish 'push and run' game, they were top of the table in September and remained in the top six places throughout the autumn, while further honours came to the club when Johnny Byrne became our first England international since May 1923 when he lined up against Northern Ireland at Wembley on 22 November.

The first game of the season was at Torquay. Torquay had finished 1960/61 in mid-table so this was a tough opening match for Palace, but with the new-look forward line blending well from the start, Palace were much the better side throughout the first half and some Palace fans came to think that this first 45 minutes of the season was actually the side's best 'half' on an away ground of the entire term. Johnny Byrne hit a post early, but was on target after a quarter of an hour, rounding the centre half then coolly thumping the ball past the exposed goalkeeper. Palace had the ball in the Torquay net twice more before the interval but were denied on each occasion for offside infringements.

Torquay played much better in the second half and Palace's defence was tested, with Vic Rouse and George Petchey both having outstanding games. But after some thirty minutes of almost ceaseless Torquay pressure the Palace set up a rare attack and Roy Summersby scored after a clever combination between Byrne and Andy Smillie.

The Gulls now realised that the day was effectively lost, but they did gain some consolation when their new outside right, Gordon Astall who had signed for them in the close season from Birmingham, headed past Vic Rouse. Encouraged, they did press hard in the closing minutes but the ultimate Palace victory was fully deserved on the ninety minutes play.

Talented Andy Smillie – Palace's
top scorer in 1961/62.

Torquay United 1
Astall

Crystal Palace 2
Byrne
Summersby

Aston Villa v. Crystal Palace

Saturday 6 January 1962
Referee: Mr L. Callaghan

FA Challenge Cup, Third Round
Attendance: 39,011

Palace twice managed to reach the third round of the FA Cup as a Fourth Division club, only then to lose narrowly on distant away grounds to unglamorous opponents, but after gaining promotion in 1961 they were involved in a magnificent Cup-tie in which the Palace team reached levels of performance unmatched by club representatives for many years previously, and only surpassed after they themselves had gained higher League status. In fact, regular Palace fans who helped to swell the crowd at Aston Villa on this cold first Saturday of 1962, remained convinced that our performance that afternoon was so outstanding that it represented our peak under manager Arthur Rowe.

Apart from its bitter finale, the entire proceedings brought enormous credit to Crystal Palace. Villa, then as now, were a leading top-flight outfit and were particularly strong at their prestigious headquarters – but they came so close not just to embarrassment but outright defeat that no fair-minded fan at Villa Park would have begrudged Palace the replay we so patently deserved.

Villa swaggered through the opening quarter of an hour, clearly believing that victory was theirs for the asking, and when they scored the first goal it seemed perhaps that this might be so, although Palace fans who were present will confirm my own certainty that its scorer, Harry Burrows, was blatantly offside.

But what followed was quite wonderful: Johnny Byrne beat Nigel Sims in spectacular fashion a few minutes later, and then Dennis Uphill put Palace ahead, despite being fouled, stabbing the ball into an empty Villa net. Eire's international winger Roy McParland headed Villa back on terms, but Palace matched their illustrious hosts skill for skill and played at such a pace that the home side were quite bemused. Early in the second half Johnny Byrne restored Palace's lead, heading a Ron Heckman cross past Sims, but Villa made it 3-3 through Derek Dougan.

Palace were now clearly the equals of Villa and the game had reached its dying moments of surprisingly extended added time when Palace conceded a killer goal. A drifting cross-cum-centre from Burrows swirled out of the mist, eluded the groping hands of Vic Rouse, and then ended up in the far corner of our net. There was barely time to restart the game before the final whistle. Palace and their fans were disappointed of course, but Palace had matched a leading, pedigree outfit on their own ground and hugely impressed all the neutral observers, so that there was considerable consolation to be gained on the journey home. But none of us knew that, if we waited long enough, there was indeed to be FA Cup glory for the Palace at Villa Park one day!

Johnny Byrne.

Aston Villa 4
Burrows (2)
Mc Parland, Dougan

Crystal Palace 3
Byrne (2)
Uphill

Wednesday 18 April 1962
Referee: Mr M. Kitabdjian (France)

Friendly Match
Attendance: 24,740

Skippers Johnny McNichol (right) and Francisco Gento exchange pennants before the kick-off.

It may seem strange to find a mere friendly match among this catalogue of classic Crystal Palace matches, but no modern-day fan should be under any illusions – this friendly match was a highly memorable, quite magnificent Palace occasion and it probably represents the biggest single club match ever played at Selhurst Park in terms of the relative value of the stars who played in it. For confirmation of that, just note even the visitors named here and remember that Real Madrid weren't only champions of Europe – they had been so for five years – a record beyond compare even today! Point made? Point taken!

Early in 1962 the Palace directors had discussed the possible clubs to invite to mark the opening of new, much improved floodlights. A big, really big, club was wanted. Certain English clubs were approached but wanted hefty guarantees on top of expenses, so our Board, under visionary chairman Arthur Wait, decided that if money of such proportions was to be involved then the opponents might as well be the club that was at that time supreme in European soccer, Real Madrid. Somehow, Mr Wait – chairman of a modest Third Division club, remember – persuaded the elite of football to make their first visit to London. The Spaniards agreed to play for £10,000: Palace put up their prices and, even though it poured with rain for eighteen hours prior to the match, they took over £15,000 and made a profit of some £3,000 for the night's venture.

Nor was it just the Palace bank manager who was happy – none of the fans who came will ever forget that evening! Cold and raw it may have been, but we were oblivious to the weather as Real paraded precisely their fabulous skills. They honoured their responsibilities to the full and paraded precisely the same side that had represented them the previous week when they had won a European Cup semi-final against Standard Liège. Palace were allowed to include Johnny Byrne as a guest after his record-breaking transfer to West Ham some six weeks earlier. Inevitably, Di Stefano, Puskas and Gento were all prominent and Real cruised to a two-goal lead in eight minutes. Ron Heckman reduced the arrears with a header from Byrne's left-footed cross but Puskas hammered a thunderous thirty-yard free kick into the net two minutes later, then Sanchez crowned a wonderful short passing move in which the Hungarian captain had again been involved with Di Stefano.

However, Palace, playing in a unique strip of claret and blue striped shirts and claret shorts, rallied well after the break: Andy Smillie prodded Roy Summersby's pass past Vicente and then Terry Long hit a 25-yarder of which Puskas himself would have been proud. 3-4 and the Spanish señores were worried! But try as Palace did, they were unable to clinch an equaliser and Real's pride remained intact.

Crystal Palace 3
Heckman
Smillie, Long

Real Madrid 4
Di Stefano, Gento
Puskas, Sanchez

CRYSTAL PALACE v. MILLWALL

Wednesday 26 December 1962
Referee: Mr G.D. Roper

Football League, Third Division
Attendance: 20,419

Peter Burridge.

At the time of this south London derby, Palace were in dire trouble and appeared to be heading for an ignominious return to the League basement we'd only managed to leave a season and a half before. The club's decline should not be solely attributed to the absence of Johnny Byrne. The whole club, but especially the players and manager Arthur Rowe, were badly affected by the tragic death of Ron Brett in a traffic accident at the end of August, and then Arthur Rowe was struck down by illness and forced to drop his responsibilities.

Dick Graham, Palace's former goalkeeper and assistant to Mr Rowe since January 1961, took over, immediately changed the style of play and made two masterly signings. Palace now adopted a much more direct game, perfectly suited to the new manager's first signings, the proven goalscorers Cliff Holton and 'Dickie' Dowsett. This Boxing Day derby was their first match together in Palace colours and Holton's debut. Millwall sought to mark him out of the game, but in doing so the Lions' defence left the way open for Palace's other forwards to cleave their way through and net three goals, something they had previously not accomplished all season.

Palace adopted a classic Dick Graham attitude: tough, man-for-man marking soon gained control. The most important duel was on Palace's left flank where Millwall's flying winger Joey Broadfoot was a constant menace, but Bert Howe gradually cut off the danger there and subsequently shadowed the Lions' star as he roamed all over the park. In the end, the Palace defence finished with a clean sheet - their first in eight games and more than welcome to everyone.

The conditions were bitterly cold and icy underfoot and on the tricky surface Palace looked the more assured. Speedy and confident, they gained the ascendancy a little after a quarter of an hour when Peter Burridge netted against his former club following a Bert Howe free kick. Early in the second half, 'Dickie' Dowsett scored his first Palace goal: reacting quickly to a Ronnie Allen through ball, he raced past a defender to turn it beyond Reg Davis in the Millwall goal. The finale was just before the end. Millwall brought down Peter Burridge in the penalty area and, although the fans called for a Cliff Holton 'special', Ronnie Allen stepped up to clip a deft shot past the goalkeeper's left hand.

Crystal Palace 3
Burridge, Dowsett
Allen (pen)

Millwall 0

Wednesday 22 April 1964   Football League, Third Division
Referee: Mr J.S. Pickles   Attendance: 3,384

By the time of this penultimate fixture of the 1963/64 season, Palace's promotion momentum was buoyant and on course. This last away game held few terrors for the experienced side – not only were Wrexham in perilous danger of relegation, but Palace were unbeaten on the road in eight trips and knew that a single point from The Racecourse would ensure promotion with one (home) game remaining, in which they could take the divisional championship.

Thus there was an understandably content and expectant air about the commendably strong group of Palace fans who had been able to make the journey while the players appeared quietly determined to do the job before them. However, whilst it would not be true to suggest that the team were affected by this occasion – with a crowd of under four thousand this was unlikely! – it would certainly be fair to say that those of us who were present recognised that Palace's performance this evening was one that was below par.

Ironically for the home side it was their former player Brian Whitehouse who generated some zest among Palace's men. The half hour was approaching, Palace has seen Bill Glazier beaten by a cleverly taken goal and they urgently needed a spark from somewhere… But then, from at least thirty yards (I am actually tempted to write 'perhaps forty', but memory has a habit of exaggerating!) Whitehouse delivered a blistering drive which ripped into the Welshmen's goal. It stunned their players, along with the home crowd.

Palace were lifted somewhat by their equaliser and soon came again – but this time Eddie Werge was pulled down in the penalty area when cutting in on goal with the ball at his feet. Cliff Holton rapped home the penalty – but only four minutes later George Petchey conceded one and Wrexham's player-manager Ken Barnes restored parity.

The second half was certainly won on points by Wrexham. Barnes was denied early on by a fabulous Glazier save; Sam McMillan headed against the Palace crossbar and in the closing stages Glazier pulled out another fine save to foil Phythian. But eventually the final whistle went. Palace had gained their point and some of the Palace fans were sufficiently jubilant to spill out onto the pitch to congratulate their heroes (though it would probably be better not to embarrass any of those who are now among our veteran supporters by naming anybody!).

Curiously, Palace's low key approach at Wrexham was carried over into the final game of the season at home to Oldham, which was lost, along with any hopes of clinching the divisional title.

Palace's team at Wrexham whose 2-2 draw gained them promotion from the Third Division.

Wrexham 2
Phythian
Barnes (pen)

Crystal Palace 2
Whitehouse
Holton (pen)

CRYSTAL PALACE v. PORTSMOUTH

Saturday 26 December 1964
Referee: Mr J. Carter

Football League, Second Division
Attendance: 18,758

David Burnside – two goals on his Palace debut.

The 1964/65 season was Palace's first in the upper divisions of the League for forty years, whereas recent top-flight regulars Portsmouth were the 'fallen giants' of the day. They had been in the Third Division with the Palace in 1961/62 and there had been three bruising matches between the clubs in League and Cup clashes that season. This Boxing Day pairing consequently created plenty of interest. The fixture was made more attractive because manager Dick Graham had actually paid a club record fee of £14,000 to Southampton when Graham's former West Bromwich Albion club-mate David Burnside joined Palace just before Christmas. He was a supremely skilled inside forward and it might be said that the tricky, icy Selhurst Park surface was precisely the sort that he would have chosen for his debut. Be that as it may, Palace provided an outstanding display, and the fans were enthralled when David prompted the side to an impressive 4-2 victory despite falling into arrears early in the game.

But, sparkling though Burnside's first Palace outing undoubtedly was, the best player of the day was actually little Bobby Kellard, whose stocky frame was ideally suited to the conditions. He was virtually unstoppable out on Palace's left flank with pace, trickery and close control that opened Pompey up time and time again.

That said, Portsmouth did start the scoring with a clever lob, but David Burnside hit a post before he equalised midway through the first half when he fastened on to a Kellard effort that was drifting wide, rounded two defenders then fired into the net. Keith Smith – the scorer of Palace's fastest ever goal just two weeks earlier – put Palace ahead early in the second half, Milkins being unable to hold his shot which slithered over the line. Alan Stephenson then stepped up to claim a rare Palace goal for himself. Pompey's John McClelland reduced their arrears, but a wonderful Palace move involving Cliff Holton, Smith and David Burnside enabled the new signing to stride through to ensure a Palace victory with some grace and style.

Palace gained a point from the return fixture at Portsmouth the following Tuesday evening when John Holsgrove opened the scoring for Palace, but Palace's former player Brian Lewis replied for Portsmouth to ensure that the honours were shared. Palace's impressive form continued throughout 1964/65, so that they finished their first season after promotion in a most praiseworthy seventh position. Pompey escaped relegation back to the Third Division by one point and one place.

Crystal Palace 4	Portsmouth 2
Burnside (2), Smith	*McCann*
Stephenson	*McClelland*

Saturday 20 February 1965
Referee: Mr K. Dagnall

FA Challenge Cup, Fifth Round
Attendance: 41,667 (new ground record)

Crystal Palace had beaten fellow Second Division sides Bury and Southampton to reach this stage of the FA Cup competition, and that in itself was a fine achievement for a club playing at this level of the League for the first time in 39 years.

In fact, in retrospect, it is possible to see that Crystal Palace at this time were at their most effective best under the management of former Palace goalkeeper Dick Graham, but, against the style and pedigree of gifted, top-flight aristocrats Nottingham Forest, Palace were emphatically the outsiders and the possibility of an upset was regarded as unlikely by the neutrals. But that is to undervalue the Palace of the day: Palace fans certainly felt the side were in with at least a chance and I travelled down overnight from Durham University for this game in evidence of that.

Possibly, Forest underestimated the size of their task. It is also possible that, like many clubs before them, they were initially puzzled by Dick Graham's 'numbers game'. Beyond dispute was the fact that in Cliff Holton, Palace possessed an inspirational centre forward who was capable of making and taking goals that could turn any game.

The match was an exhilarating one, played on a heavy, snow-flecked pitch and on a cold, late winter's afternoon. Every Palace man was a hero, although I thought Alan Stephenson Palace's outstanding player as he largely extinguished the threat of the current England centre forward Frank Wignall. Palace showed no respect whatsoever for Forest's class; indeed it was a fair reflection of the first-half balance of play when, in the 41st minute, Roy Horobin flicked a low pass out to Bobby Kellard and David Burnside was first to the cross to deliver a refined header just inside the far post.

Forest demonstrated their calibre after the break when Wignall forced home an equaliser after Henry Newton had hit a post and for a quarter of an hour this enthralling game was in the balance. But the Palace then netted with a superb goal whose power and pace typified the side's style and character at that time. Burnside liberated Cliff Holton who hammered a cross from the left for Peter Burridge to volley gloriously, left-footed, past the helpless goalkeeper.

Five minutes from time, any doubts as to the outcome were stifled when Cliff Holton scored from close range with Forest's tiring defence completely exposed and Palace were in the FA Cup quarter-finals for the first time since 1907!

Cliff Holton is the subject of this Jim Mercer cartoon.

Crystal Palace 3
Burnside, Burridge
Holton

Nottingham Forest 1
Wignall

BIRMINGHAM CITY v. CRYSTAL PALACE

Saturday 21 August 1965
Referee: Mr W. Crossley

Football League, Second Division
Attendance: 19,205

Palace proved to be a mid-table Second Division side throughout 1965/66, which was to be the last in which Dick Graham took charge as manager. His departure in January 1966 had little or no effect upon the club's playing record, but this opening match of the term was to show Palace at their most resilient under his new management even if it was to finish in bizarre circumstances which remained unique at the club for over thirty years.

This first game was undoubtedly a tough one. Palace were at St Andrews, the home of Birmingham City, who had been relegated from the top flight the previous April. Keith Smith hit a post for Palace early on with goalkeeper Jim Herriott out of position, then David Burnside revealed a previously undisclosed talent when shepherding a small dog out of the action after the little canine had strayed into the arena! But moments after this 'success', Palace were in arrears when Bert Howe had difficulty with a long headed pass, was dispossessed by Dennis Thwaites and saw the Blues' striker find the net despite John Jackson getting a hand to the shot.

Under Dick Graham, Palace were never short of tenacity and they were level four minutes before half time. Burnside gained possession and found debutant centre forward Ian Lawson with an adroit pass that enabled the former Leeds man space and time to hit the ball powerfully towards the goal. Herriott managed to put a hand to the ball as it passed him but the deflection only served to lift it high into the roof of the net.

Birmingham restored their advantage late on in the proceedings, but in the last moments Palace gained a corner and Alan Stephenson leapt high at the far post to nod the ball home. However, while the ball was still in flight and before it had crossed the goal-line, the referee began to blow his whistle for the end of the match and, although the ball hit the back of the net while he was still blowing, the 'goal' could not stand, for it is the first note of the final whistle that signals the close of the game.

Today's readers will probably recall the occasion when Palace suffered again in the same way. Portsmouth were the visitors on Saturday 23 March 1966 and were hanging on for a tedious draw when Eagles skipper Andy Roberts let fly with a thirty-yard drive that billowed the Holmesdale Road netting, but the referee had blown for time as the ball left Andy's foot.

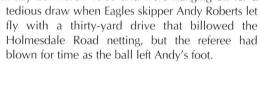

Alan Stephenson's 'equaliser' came a moment too late.

Birmingham City 2
Thwaites (2)

Crystal Palace 1
Lawson

CRYSTAL PALACE v. WOLVERHAMPTON WANDERERS

Saturday 13 May 1967
Referee: Mr E.D. Wallace

Football League, Second Division
Attendance: 26,930

Jackie Bannister.

The 1966/67 season was Bert Head's first full term in charge at Selhurst Park and it had proved highly encouraging for everyone at Crystal Palace FC. It came to its conclusion on the humid, heavy middle Saturday of May (its start having been delayed for a couple of weeks after the 1966 World Cup) when Palace were favoured with the most interesting match of the afternoon – they were at home to Wolves who were top of the table, certain of promotion and within a single point of the Second Division championship.

Interest was significantly added for all Palace fans because Wolves were managed by our former skipper, England star Ronnie Allen, and the side included two former Palace men, sophisticated midfielder David Burnside (who had moved to Molineux early in the season and made his Wolves debut against the Palace!) and the towering centre half or defensive midfielder John Holsgrove.

To say that Palace beat Wolves this afternoon is to come nowhere near the full reality: we outplayed them in every department and throughout the game so that there was no doubt that this performance was Palace's best at Selhurst Park of 1966/67, although it may have been shaded by the 2-1 win at eventual champions Coventry six months earlier in the Sky Blues' only home defeat of the term.

Palace's inspiration on this occasion was Johnny Byrne, who had returned to the club from West Ham the previous February and this game was his best in in his second spell with the side. He was simply too clever for the Wolves defence and combined effectively with recent newcomer to the side Danny Light.

In fact it was Light who made Palace's intentions clear early in the contest, driving the ball into the netting to capitalise on a Byrne-Cliff Jackson opening. Palace fans' delight was increased as the half hour approached and Bobby Woodruff headed a John Sewell lob past Phil Parkes and against his own former club, to record his sixth goal in five games. Just as the hour passed it was all over; Jackie Bannister took a pass from Light, broke clear, then unleashed a spectacular long-range drive that was still rising when it entered the net just inside the post. Wolves rallied sufficiently to restore a little dignity with a quality goal, but Palace had the last word when Barry Dyson confirmed their superiority on the day, rounded off a fine victory and stated Palace's own firm intentions of joining Wolves in the top flight as quickly as possible. It is interesting, however, that when they did manage to do this, two years later, only four members of the successful side against Wolves would play significant parts in the Palace squad that did so.

Crystal Palace 4
Light, Woodruff
Bannister, Dyson

Wolverhampton Wanderers 1
Hunt

CRYSTAL PALACE v. QUEENS PARK RANGERS

Saturday 30 September 1967
Referee: Mr C. Nicholls

Football League, Second Division
Attendance: 38,006

After finishing 1966/67 on such a positive note, Palace continued in fine form at the opening of 1967/68 and by the end of September, following a midweek Selhurst Park victory over mid-table Cardiff, we were placed right on the shoulder of top club Queens Park Rangers – who were due to be Palace's next opponents here on the last day of the month!

Inevitably the contest created enormous interest among football fans in south and west London and, helped by the bright, warm early autumn afternoon, it drew the biggest attendance Selhurst Park had ever hosted for a League game up to that time.

Palace had been absolutely invincible at home thus far and had conceded just one goal while securing five straight victories, but this favourable portent had to be measured against an extended injury list which saw the side without captain Alan Stephenson, his deputy Johnny Byrne or regular left winger Cliff Jackson. Fortunately, however, John Sewell was able to return after missing three games and this freed Terry Long from defensive duties for a more enterprising midfield role.

Terry in fact wore the number 11 shirt for the first time in his illustrious Palace career – and for reasons which are about to become evident, everyone was very happy for him to do so on subsequent occasions too!

Because there was so much local prestige at stake, the match was quickly tough and tense with neither side willing to concede the least advantage to their opponents. The fans of both (unsegregated in those days, of course) were in fine voice. The initiative ebbed and flowed and it was soon evident that little would separate the teams. Ultimately, the outcome was settled after thirty-eight minutes with a well-worked Palace goal created by a Bobby Woodruff long throw and Tom White which presented Terry Long with the opportunity he gleefully accepted to crack the ball high into Rangers net past England international goalkeeper Ron Springett from close range.

Scoring matters remained unchanged for the rest of the afternoon which, to the enormous delight and pride of all Palace fans, was sufficient to put us ahead of Rangers and at the top of the Second Division table for the first time in our history, although it must be admitted that this was only a temporary situation, as Rangers won the Loftus Road return in February (2-1), and gained promotion at the end of the season while Palace finished in eleventh place.

Terry Long netted the goal that beat QPR and took Palace to the top of the Second Division for the first time.

Crystal Palace 1
Long

Queens Park Rangers 0

Wednesday 5 March 1969
Referee: Mr H.W. Ellis

Football League, Second Division
Attendance: 31,748

Bobby Woodruff.

The 1968/69 season suffered badly as a result of a spell of intensely cold weather which put the fixture list 'on hold' virtually everywhere throughout late January and early mid February. However, no one at Crystal Palace FC was complaining about the congested programme of matches that ensued because after the enforced break Palace were in fine form and a sixteen-match unbeaten run took us to promotion to the top flight.

Early in the revised sequence of matches, Palace achieved two stunning away victories which completely altered not just the top quarter of the Second Division table, but the whole attitude of everyone at Selhurst Park because they demonstrated that we were perfectly capable of beating the top teams in the section and could therefore make an indelible mark upon the rest of the season. First came the match under review here, a midweek rearranged game at table-topping Derby County. The Rams were unbeaten at The Baseball Ground in sixteen League games and had beaten top-flight Everton and Chelsea in League Cup ties here, but Palace were quite unimpressed by such an imposing record and over-ran their hosts to such an extent that, whilst only one counted, Palace actually netted five times!

Before their fiery supporters, Derby pressed strongly at the start of each half, but Palace, adopting an adventurous 4-2-4 formation, harried, chased and ran at their opponents for every ball. The speed and power of wingers Mark Lazarus and Colin Taylor clearly unsettled County and the wiles of Bobby Woodruff at least equalled those of Derby's own sophisticates, Alan Durban, Alan Hinton and Kevin Hector. Bobby thought he'd scored midway through the first half, but the strike was disallowed for a much earlier offside where the referee hadn't noticed his linesman's flag. Minutes later, a Woodruff header rebounded off the crossbar, and early in the second half Tony Taylor handled the ball into Derby's net.

Taylor was adjudged to have used his arm in netting again early in the second half but the moment that decided the outcome – and, arguably, set Palace on course for promotion – arrived seconds after the hour. Shots from Colin Taylor, then Tony Taylor were blocked by desperate defenders but the ball fell for Bobby Woodruff who poked it past Les Green with delight as well as aplomb. Bobby netted again soon afterwards but was ruled offside.

Derby had little response to offer and their big crowd was quiet as the proceedings drew to a close, but the amusing point of interest after the game was that John Jackson, who had been concussed in a Derby raid before Palace scored, was unaware that we had won until he was told, and then persuaded so, in the dressing-room!

Derby County 0

Crystal Palace 1
Woodruff

CRYSTAL PALACE v. FULHAM

Saturday 19 April 1969   Football League, Second Division
Referee: Mr H. New   Attendance: 36,126

Put bluntly, judged on its pure footballing merits, this game would not class as a classic. But because of the issue that hung upon its outcome it will forever be regarded as one of the most momentous in the history of our club. As the culmination of a 14-match unbeaten run and barring a disaster here, Palace were on their way to the top flight for the first time ever, while their opponents, Fulham, were in bottom place and already doomed to relegation.

But the Cottagers simply hadn't read the script! They were the better team throughout the first half and came in at the break deservedly two goals ahead. Former Palace star Johnny Byrne had initiated both: a surprise opener from Brian Dear, half an hour later, another from Frank Large.

During the interval Palace coach George Petchey gave the players the benefit of a few home truths and his pep talk reaped rapid dividends, for Palace netted within fifty seconds of the restart. Tony Taylor raced through the middle, goalkeeper Jack McClelland was unable to hold his fierce drive and the ball ran to Steve Kember, who sharply touched it home. Now the Palace pulses quickened. Cliff Jackson might have equalised almost immediately but the second goal wasn't long delayed. It came from Mark Lazarus, with a twenty-yard drive in the 59th minute after incisive play from Colin Taylor and Cliff Jackson and, typically, Mark set off on one of his extended celebrations which finished at the other end with an embrace for John Jackson. And just three minutes later Palace were in front! Colin Taylor and Roger Hoy built a move which set Cliff Jackson free and the centre forward speared his shot high into the corner of the net, before raising his arm in his characteristic warrior's salute.

After these amazing seventeen minutes, the match eased to its close, but the scenes that followed the final whistle were incredible. There have been similar ones since, of course – read on and you'll discover them all – but because this was the first time that Palace had gained promotion to the elite, they were unique. A surge of fans engulfed the pitch, the players, the officials and the police. There was jubilation everywhere and the occasion became a carnival as the triumphant Palace team appeared in the director's box and threw their shirts and other assorted items of clothing to the ecstatic and appreciative throng.

Centre spread of the Palace programme, 19 April 1969.

Crystal Palace 3
Kember, Lazarus
C. Jackson

Fulham 2
Dear
Large

CRYSTAL PALACE v. MANCHESTER UNITED

Saturday 9 August 1969
Referee: Mr H. New

Football League, First Division
Attendance: 48,610 (new ground record)

John Jackson pushes away a shot from Denis Law, with John McCormick watching closely.

This fixture was Palace's first ever game in the top flight of English League football and, until recent years, took place on the earliest date for the opening of a Football League season (in order to provide a little extra time for preparation for the World Cup Finals to be held the following summer in Mexico). It could scarcely have created greater interest if the club had been allowed to choose its own opponents for the occasion because Palace had been favoured with home advantage and our visitors were Manchester United – then, as now, an illustrious club and the one above all other that everyone wanted to see.

The day was a classic one for the first day of a new football season – hot, humid and sunny! Regardless of the date, how often does that seem to be the case? Despite being slap bang in the middle of the holiday season, this unique fixture drew a (then) record crowd to Selhurst Park and generated record receipts of £16,250. The fans were certainly treated to an exciting afternoon's entertainment, even if, like so many emotion charged games, the match fell some way short of being a masterpiece.

Palace's line-up for the big opener included two new signings. Stylish striker Gerry Queen had joined the club from Kilmarnock and he was to prove probably manager Bert Head's best acquisition over the four years in the First Division between 1969 and 1973 when he was easily our top goalscorer and his tally of 18 in the first two seasons represented precisely one quarter of Palace's total. Tall, dark, muscular defender Roger Hynd had come from Rangers to play

Crystal Palace 2
Blyth
Queen

Manchester United 2
Charlton
Morgan

CRYSTAL PALACE v. MANCHESTER UNITED

Palace debutant Roger Hynd.

alongside evergreen centre half John McCormick. Immensely powerful, Roger was an initial asset but as the season developed so Mel Blyth's capacities became the better suited to the purely defensive role and Roger's value to Palace became less obvious, although on this particular occasion he certainly played his part in ensuring our point and he did prove of real use as a battering ram centre forward in some later matches – see the next match report for a perfect example!

Matters had not been under way for long when Palace edged in front, but many London-based observers who were present were surprised to witness a team of United's calibre fall for Palace's well-established, rehearsed and publicised long throw-in routine. This had reaped huge dividends for the club in the lower division, but few of us were expecting it to prove quite so productive so early in our top-flight tenure. Roger Hoy's delivery was met by Mel Blyth, whose header looped over United's Jimmy Rimmer (who was under pressure from Roger Hynd) and then dipped into the untenanted net! Mel had an excellent match, coping admirably with the demands posed by Bobby Charlton, but such things fade so easily from the memory, whereas the eternal statistic remains that his splendid performance was crowned with Palace's first ever goal in the top flight.

Inevitably perhaps, since Bobby Charlton's supreme talent could never be completely submerged, the England star had United level midway through the first hand when he whacked a cross from Willie Morgan past a startled John Jackson. United dominated most of the first half play after this but Palace's passion proved invaluable and as the interval approached the momentum of the game swung again, this time in our favour with Gerry Queen's goal on his Palace debut. Gerry evaded David Sadler then beat Rimmer with his shot to create pandemonium around Selhurst Park.

The second half saw United lay siege to the Palace goal and no-one could deny that the visitors deserved Willie Morgan's leveller, but the stifling humidity clearly took its toll in the later stages and United now appeared quite content, with their dignity intact and a point from their first game.

For Palace and their supporters, it had been a great day. They had been paired with one of the best teams in the land and had held their own. They may not have been able to match United for artistry and sophistication but they had made up for that by prodigious running, covering and sheer hard work – and made it abundantly clear that no club could expect an easy ride when their turn came to visit Palace's headquarters.

Crystal Palace: J. Jackson, Sewell, Loughlan, Hoy, McCormick, Hynd, Lazarus (sub T. Taylor 86) Kember, C. Jackson, Queen, Blyth.
Manchester United: Rimmer, Dunne (sub Givens) Burns, Crerand, Foulkes, Sadler, Morgan, Kidd, Charlton, Law, Best.

CRYSTAL PALACE v. TOTTENHAM HOTSPUR

Wednesday 28 January 1970
Referee: Mr V. James

FA Challenge Cup, Fourth Round Replay
Attendance: 45,980

During Palace's initial four-year top-flight tenure, the club received a great deal of adverse publicity concerning our unfortunate inability to beat First Division London opponents. As so often though, the media would not allow an inconvenient fact to detract from an easy story – because Palace had beaten Tottenham in a magnificent fourth round FA Cup replay in their first season at the highest level and would go on to gain an even bigger Capital scalp ten months later in another fabulous Cup tie victory.

So, perhaps belatedly, but with enormous pleasure, now's the opportunity to set the record straight! Palace had secured an unexpected moral victory four days earlier on a White Hart Lane glue-pot of a pitch where, without ever really troubling Spurs themselves, Palace had reduced them and their fans to such frustration that the north Londoners in the crowd had slow handclapped some of the proceedings. Now, however, at Selhurst Park, there was no such restraint. With nothing to lose, Bert Head realised that Tottenham might prove vulnerable to an all out attacking, action-based performance, so Palace lined up with *four* outright attackers – and even kept to this system when they lost central defender John McCormick with a broken nose after only twenty minutes. Playing alongside Gerry Queen and Cliff Jackson were the strong, powerful Roger Hynd and Roger Hoy – the latter, a former Spurs player, had a fantastic night against his old pals. Gerry Queen revelled in the support he had not previously received all season and adopted a shoot on sight policy which placed the Tottenham defence under constant threat and strain.

John Sewell was an inspirational skipper; this was just the sort of battle that he revelled in while John Jackson made two important saves when Palace were adjusting to the loss of McCormick. But the match was won and lost in the first quarter of an hour after the break. Palace came out like a buffalo stampede and simply ground down Tottenham's effete resistance. The hour was approaching when Tony Taylor speared the ball deep into the Tottenham penalty area where he had spotted that Gerry Queen was unmarked and Gerry delivered the *coup de grâce* with a stylish, glancing header past Pat Jennings to which Spurs found themselves quite unable to respond, while Palace might have added to their slender lead.

And that demonstrates for modern day Palace fans just why the press and television jibes of the early 1970s rankled so much with their predecessors!

Cliff Jackson.

Crystal Palace 1
   Queen

Tottenham Hotspur 0

CRYSTAL PALACE v. MANCHESTER CITY

Monday 6 April 1970
Referee: Mr E. Wallace

Football League, First Division
Attendance: 27,704

This was Palace's final First Division fixture of 1969/70, despite being played as early as the first week in April, but it could have been the club's nemesis. Palace and their fans knew that a victory here was essential in order to make more difficult the task of the two other clubs who could be relegated, Sunderland and Sheffield Wednesday. Palace had gained their only away victory of the First Division term at Maine Road, but, without a win in their last six outings and two demoralising defeats at Arsenal (2-0) and Liverpool (3-0) in the previous two games, they were in a desperate position.

Nevertheless, and despite a somewhat under-strength City line-up, Palace made light of the heavy pitch and were by far the better team. Palace's priceless goal came after twenty-one minutes: Gerry Queen was fouled; Steve Kember took a well-rehearsed free kick from which Cliff Jackson found Queen whose short cross was crashed home ecstatically from some six yards by Roger Hoy. This was Roger's last Palace game – he joined Luton in the summer – but his goal typified his near two-year spell with Palace, in which he helped the side to first gain promotion, and then to retain their elite status.

But, as so often in the club's top flight days of 1969 to 1973, Palace owed a considerable debt to goalkeeper John Jackson, who made brilliant second-half saves to deny first a Chris Glennon header and then an Alan Oakes volley to protect Palace's precious lead. Palace drew inspiration and courage from 'Jacko's' magnificent display to defy the visitors to the end.

Upon the final whistle, the Palace supporters stormed across the pitch to acclaim the side, confident that our survival had been ensured, but the fact was that that depended now upon whether either of our partners in distress could claim three points from their two outstanding games. Bert Head considered that he 'would rather have the three points than two games to play' and, thankfully, so it proved, although it was not until another sixteen days had elapsed that Palace's reprieve was finally assured after the Owls lost 2-1 at home to Manchester City in a Hillsborough match attended by several Palace fans.

Roger Hoy scored a crucial goal in his last Palace game.

Crystal Palace 1
Hey

Manchester City 0

MANCHESTER UNITED v. CRYSTAL PALACE

Saturday 10 October 1970
Referee: Mr R.B. Kirkpatrick

Football League, First Division
Attendance: 42,979

Bobby Tambling.

Palace travelled to Old Trafford a stronger and more confident side than the 1969/70 team which had narrowly escaped relegation. However, they were still expected, certainly by the northern media, merely to provide the opposition for Bobby Charlton's 500th League appearance for Manchester United. This matter was given added zest because Bobby also needed just one goal to pass the United record of 198 League and Cup goals set by his predecessor Jack Rowley.

But Palace now possessed an ace goalscorer themselves in the shape of Bobby Tambling, who had signed in the close season from Chelsea after an impressive loan spell the previous January.

However, no fixture at Old Trafford in any generation is anything but onerous and if United were not at this time quite the force they had once been and would again become, this match still had 'home banker' written all over it – except in the reckoning of the Palace players, manager and loyal fans who made the long journey.

Once United's early, frenetic pressure had been stemmed, Palace gradually asserted themselves. True, as expected, the England luminary was able to deliver a couple of his trademark thunderbolts, but these were deflected away from the target by watchful, close-marking defenders and John Jackson in the Palace goal was untroubled by them. In fact, by the interval, it was apparent that the Palace were perfectly capable of springing the shock result of the day for United's midfield was in thrall of Steve Kember and David Payne while Mel Blyth and John McCormick were outstanding at the heart of our defence.

In fact only several fine saves from Jimmy Rimmer had thwarted the Palace strikers, but even Rimmer had no answer just after the hour. A swift overlap on the Palace left by Peter Wall caught United's men unawares and his pass to Bobby Tambling was struck perfectly from the edge of the penalty area to give the goalkeeper no chance and record a goal that was worthy of Charlton himself. United never seriously threatened after this and Palace undoubtedly deserved their success, even if before the start such an outcome had seemed most unlikely!

Manchester United 0

Crystal Palace 1
Tambling

Monday 9 November 1970
Referee: Mr N. Burtenshaw

Football League Cup, Fourth Round Replay
Attendance: 45,026

Tony Taylor.

David Payne.

Given Arsenal's supreme pedigree in what was a fabulous season for them, this result certainly classed as a huge shock to the footballing public of London and of the entire First Division fraternity as a whole. It would have appeared that Palace's chance of springing a surprise and progressing to the quarter-finals of the League Cup at the Gunners' expense had been lost when Arsenal secured a 0-0 draw at Selhurst Park twelve days earlier, and since Palace were missing Mel Blyth and Steve Kember, such hopes as Palace fans entertained upon arrival at Highbury were, initially at least, somewhat forced.

Of course, and as expected, Palace were under a lot, indeed, at times, intense, pressure but we defended magnificently in the face of Arsenal's ceaseless raids and it was perhaps an indication of the home side's over confidence that they squandered several gilt-edged chances. Thus, not even the most zealous Palace partisan could argue that it was not against the run of play when Jim Scott's shot was misfielded by Bob Wilson after a quarter of an hour and Gerry Queen tucked away the rebound.

With John Sewell having to be replaced by John Loughlan soon afterwards, it seemed impossible that Palace could hold on to their lead, let alone add to it! But with a quarter of an hour to go and Arsenal's huge crowd in a near frenzy, their burly Welsh international defender John Roberts showed his frustration by manhandling Gerry Queen and Bobby Tambling rifled the spot kick home to emphasise our resilience and maturity at this time and provide the club's biggest shock result during its first tenure in the First Division between 1969 and 1973.

Arsenal's own programme, for Palace's League fixture at Highbury the following Saturday (1-1), was honest and sporting in the finest traditions of that club: 'Palace, not at full strength and with their captain having to be substituted in the first half, must be given credit for winning as they did'. The Gunners' official scribe didn't have to write in such vein again that season for Arsenal remained unbeaten at home after this and went on to win the 'double'. Such was the magnitude of this Palace victory.

Arsenal 0

Crystal Palace 2
Queen
Tambling (pen)

CRYSTAL PALACE v. LIVERPOOL

Saturday 16 January 1971
Referee: Mr H. Williams

Football League, First Division
Attendance: 28,253

Palace's second season among the elite had started well, although by mid-term they had slipped back into mid-table. This was somewhat galling for the home fans in particular, who had not seen them win at Selhurst Park in seven League and Cup matches since mid-October, even if visiting Liverpool knew Palace had only lost once here since their opening home game.

Now, whilst any Palace victory over the Reds from Merseyside is of course greatly to be welcomed and cheered, present day fans should know that at this time there had not yet developed the passionate rivalry that we feel towards Liverpool today. The victory we gained was a prestigious one, certainly – but the reasons for its inclusion here are both historic and personal. It was Palace's first win over Liverpool, and, as a youthful curate in Liverpool diocese at that time, much credibility hung over me upon the outcome! So, imagine my delight when the lads from Skelmersdale who had travelled down for the game rang me to tell me the scoreline – and to announce that I had been featured as Palace's 'Fan of the Week' in the match-day programme!

The decisive moment came right on the hour when an eighth consecutive home draw had begun to appear likely, but John Sewell hoisted a cross into Liverpool's goalmouth. Alan Birchenall bravely defied the challenge of Chris Lawler and Ray Clemence's flailing fists to get his head to it. The ball deflected upwards, then dropped towards the goal where Gerry Queen – much admired and indeed sought after by Liverpool boss Bill Shankly – raced in ahead of all challengers to touch it over the line and into the net for his tenth strike of the season. Birchenall and Lawler were both prone and unconscious after clashing heads and there was some delay while they received the necessary attention to revive them.

It has to be said that Liverpool were not yet quite the force that they were soon to become. They would finish 1970/71 in fifth place in the First Division, but this was nevertheless a well deserved victory for our club and it did mean that Palace took three points out of the four from 'Pool that season.

Not that the win was easily achieved. Liverpool's response to falling into arrears was precisely what modern day fans would have expected from them, and Palace had to defend against sustained pressure for long periods against their star-laden side. But the side did so with impressive resilience and enthusiasm, with perhaps Mel Blyth and Phil Hoadley the most outstanding, plus, inevitably, John Jackson, who made superb saves from a John Toshack header and at close range from Steve Heighway.

Gerry Queen scores the goal that defeated Liverpool.

Crystal Palace 1
   Queen

Liverpool 0

CRYSTAL PALACE v. SHEFFIELD UNITED

Saturday 4 December 1971
Referee: Mr R. Capey

Football League, First Division
Attendance: 20,176

Crystal Palace only scored more than four goals on two occasions during their top-flight tenure of 1969 to 1973. This fixture was the first of them and it is naturally a game about which the fans of that period frequently reminisce. Yet, curiously, the Palace player whose performance did most to bring about this stunning victory is not one whose name appears often in lists of great stars of the club. His name was John Hughes. Strapping, fast-running and a powerful attacker, the Scottish international was a great bear of a man who had been nicknamed 'Yogi' after the cartoon character of the time by his fans at his former club, Celtic. The sobriquet followed him to Selhurst Park when Bert Head signed him as part of that manager's first and successful restructuring plan in the autumn of 1971 following a poor start to that season.

It was a clever signing and John might have become a prolific scorer for the Palace but he was badly injured late in this game after having run riot among the Blades' defenders, scored two magnificent goals and inspired Palace to a comprehensive, morale-raising victory.

Palace were rock-bottom of the table at the time of this match: United were fourth (though it has to be said they were poor travellers) and had hit seven goals the previous weekend, so the portents were decidedly ominous! But with another of Mr Head's new signings, Bobby Kellard, having a superb game in midfield, Palace completely overwhelmed their visitors, and the match was already well won inside the first half hour!

Tony Taylor clipped Palace's early opener past John Hope following a quickly taken Gerry Queen free kick and two minutes later John Hughes signalled the coming of the avalanche. Receiving from Queen, he flicked the ball over Len Badger, charged into the penalty area and hammered a left-footed shot inside the near post. United knew that this was not to be their day just after midway through the first half when a Gerry Queen shot was deflected past Hope.

Palace's second half brace were quite brilliant. Showing his contempt for some heavy tackles, Hughes took possession on the halfway line and powered past three challenges before slamming a swerving thirty-yarder past Hope, then, after Dearden's consolation for the Blades, John McCormick netted another glorious strike from some twenty-five yards. After this performance, you could certainly say that Palace's 1971/72 recovery was under way!

John Hughes ran riot against Sheffield United.

Crystal Palace 5
T. Taylor, Hughes (2)
Queen, McCormick

Sheffield United 1
Dearden

Tuesday 11 April 1972
Referee: Mr K. Burns

Football League, First Division
Attendance: 34,384

Bobby Kellard sends Bob Wilson the wrong way from the penalty spot.

Palace's 1971/72 recovery was indeed underway in December…but their ultimate survival became a perilously close run thing. By mid April, Palace were hovering just above the two relegation places, a poor sequence of results having produced just one League victory in three months and thirteen outings. The club's next fixture was this one, at home to Arsenal. Four minutes into it, Palace were two goals in arrears.

Now, modern readers need to be assured that there was no neighbourly assistance being offered by the London rivals: for Palace to claw a way back into this game and to finally wrest a point from it was a momentous achievement. In fact, in retrospect it became possible to see that it was this recovery which gave our club renewed belief and a momentum from which sufficient further points were won to enable the club to survive by a four-point margin.

Palace's revival began in the nineteenth minute, when, under no pressure at all, defender Peter Simpson handled the ball on the side of the penalty area. Skipper Bobby Kellard, one of four mid-season signings by Bert Head in a major restructuring programme, and, arguably, the most significant of them, stepped up to flight the kick low and left-footed into the Whitehorse Lane netting while sending Bob Wilson the wrong way. Bobby proved an inspirational captain upon his arrival. He missed just one game in the remainder of the season and this goal was one of three penalties he converted for the club in the last month of it, two of which were crucial. Industrious and skilful, Bobby was the midfield inspiration for the Palace as they battled their way to eventual safety.

Palace's deserved equaliser arrived just before the hour. Bobby Kellard delivered an in-swinging corner which deceived Wilson, and John Craven lunged forward to head the ball home. John was a clever forward. He could play either as an out and out striker or in a wider role on the right. He joined the club at the same time as Kellard and featured in every remaining match, scoring seven vital First Division goals. He might have had another this evening against Arsenal, but Wilson redeemed himself with a point blank save to deny him.

The fever pitch battle continued until the end, by which time both sides were content with the outcome, but for Palace this was the night when they regained the courage to earn their continued top-flight existence and it was one of those occasions when the team and the fans gelled into a productive and exciting partnership.

Crystal Palace 2
Kellard (pen)
Craven

Arsenal 2
Radford
Ball

CRYSTAL PALACE v. MANCHESTER UNITED

Saturday 16 December 1972
Referee: Mr J. Hunting

Football League, First Division
Attendance: 39,484

At the time of this fixture, it is probably no surprise to learn that Palace were battling to climb clear of the relegation places. Manager Bert Head had sought to strengthen his squad by importing midfielder Charlie Cooke and full-back Paddy Mulligan from Chelsea, midfield or central defender Iain Philip from Dundee, mercurial striker Don Rogers from Swindon Town, and now, set for his Palace debut, another striker in Alan Whittle of Everton.

Perhaps more surprising though, is the fact that Manchester United were also in the mire at the foot of the table. Just two places and two points better off than bottom club Palace, but having played a game more, they were having a thoroughly disappointing season. Meanwhile, for this game they were missing their two great luminaries, Bobby Charlton, who had gone down with flu, and George Best, who was suspended. Even so, with their galaxy of star players, United were expected to earn at least a draw at Selhurst Park, where they had dropped just one point in their previous three top-flight visits since Palace's elevation in 1969.

United were first to threaten as a long cross from Tony Dunne from the left reached Ian Moore some ten yards out with only John Jackson left to beat. However, 'Jacko' was quickly off his line to smother the shot and a minute later Palace were ahead. Incredibly, it was right back and captain Paddy Mulligan who began the downfall of the Old Trafford sophisticates, racing on to a Don Rogers' pass which bisected two defenders on the right flank, then cutting in to steer the ball right-footed past Alex Stepney, the former Millwall goalkeeper, from an acute angle and into the Whitehorse Lane goal.

It was all Palace for a while now and Whittle might have added a quick second had Stepney not tipped a fierce drive over the bar. Denis Law came on as substitute for Eire defender Tony Dunne, who had been injured while vainly trying to halt the progress for Palace's goal, and United certainly missed his experience as the match progressed. Mel Blyth hammered a shot

Don Rogers rounds Alex Stepney in the course of scoring Palace's third goal.

Crystal Palace 5
Mulligan (2)
Rogers (2), Whittle

Manchester United 0

CRYSTAL PALACE v. MANCHESTER UNITED

All of the Palace side which trounced United feature in this team picture except for debutant Alan Whittle.

over the top, Stepney again saved well from Whittle from close range before Tony O'Neil cleared off the line from John Hughes after the big Scotsman had rounded Stepney.

Ted MacDougal did net for United, but was palpably offside before Palace increased their lead three minutes before the interval. Again, amazingly, Mulligan was the scorer, lashing the ball home unmarked from twelve yards, from Don Rogers' made-to-measure pass. Ian Moore shot narrowly over Jacko's bar immediately after the restart, but, in the 46th minute, Palace went further ahead. Alan Whittle played a perfect pass through the middle for Don Rogers to collect on the edge of the penalty area and round Stepney one way whilst pushing the ball the other side of the beleaguered keeper. He then drove it low into the untenanted Holmesdale Road netting. 'Yogi' Hughes and Charlie Cooke continued to carve great gaps in United's defence while John Jackson, so often Palace's overworked saviour in the past, was having one of the quietest afternoon's of his top-flight career, and some of the sparkle went out of the game as Palace relaxed. This was only temporary and the *coup de grâce* was yet to come!

With four minutes remaining, Alan Whittle scored the debut goal both he and the crowd craved, turning and then curling a right-footed beauty round Stepney and into the top corner from the edge of the penalty area. Then, with Palace fans' bays of 'we want five' and United in disarray, Don Rogers cut through the visitors again, rounded Stepney once more and calmly obliged.

The short-term implications of the result were to lift Palace three places, dump United next to bottom and see the Old Trafford board dismiss their manager, Frank O'Farrell, and his coaching team three days later. However, Palace were never able to build upon this victory and, despite a boardroom upheaval and management change in which Malcolm Allison was appointed Palace boss at the end of March, Palace finished the season next to bottom and were relegated. United, three places higher, survived, although they followed Palace down into the Second Division twelve months later.

Crystal Palace: Jackson, Mulligan (captain), T. Taylor, Philip, Bell, Blyth, Hughes, Payne, Whittle, Cooke, Rogers.
Manchester United: Stepney, O'Neil, Dunne (sub Law 14), Young, Sadler, Buchan (captain), Morgan, MacDougal, Kidd, Davies, Moore

CRYSTAL PALACE v. CHELSEA

Saturday 31 March 1973   Football League, First Division
Referee: Mr E. Wallace   Attendance: 39,325

Jim Cannon.

The story of this match is much, much more than simply a commendable victory over more senior London rivals: anyone who was present at it will confirm that it was an occasion dominated by big personalities and the beginning of a new Palace era. Yet, sadly, it proved to be an isolated success – indeed, within thirteen months Palace's future was destined for the third division and, within an historical perspective certainly, that fact casts a shadow across this splendid result.

On the day of course, our early excitement was compounded by an excellent Palace performance, itself emphasised by two exemplary goals, so that all Palace fans left Selhurst Park in a high state of real exultation.

Following an appalling sequence of results earlier in March, from which Palace gained just two points from six games, our club was locked into a titanic struggle for survival and on Friday 30 March the board of directors took the bold step of appointing Malcolm Allison as team manager, with Bert Head moving upstairs as general manager. The following afternoon Allison strode to the centre circle like a matador before the match, flanked by chairman Ray Bloye and Bert Head, to be hailed by the Palace faithful and inspire his new charges to record the club's first (indeed, only) top-flight win over London opponents in thirty-two attempts.

The victory was fully deserved over an admittedly injury-ridden Chelsea for whom (briefly) former Palace favourite Steve Kember was by far the best player. Palace led on the half hour. Iain Philip's initial shot was blocked but the ball was retrieved and slipped back to him by Martin Hinshelwood and the Scottish Under 23 star smacked a twenty-five yard beauty into the top corner of the net. But the best for Palace was yet to come!

Nineteen-year-old Glaswegian Jim Cannon had only been told some ninety minutes before the game that he would be making his senior Palace debut, but his performance was quite outstanding. Not only did he shackle a seemingly lethargic Peter Osgood, but he scored Palace's crucial second goal. Eleven minutes into the second half and with Chelsea girding themselves in the quest of an equaliser, Palace had a free kick. David Payne tapped the ball forward for Don Rogers to curve the ball over the Blues' wall to the far post, where young Jim had taken up an intelligent position. He soared fast and high to beat challenging defenders to the cross and headed the ball down for a fine goal to ensure Palace's eventual and long overdue success.

Regrettably, another dismal run of results consigned Palace to relegation – but there were other glories in store, as we shall soon see.

Crystal Palace 2   **Chelsea 0**
Philip
Cannon

Leeds United v. Crystal Palace

Saturday 24 January 1976
Referee: Mr K. Burns

FA Challenge Cup, Fourth Round
Attendance: 43,116

Third Division Crystal Palace had knocked out Walton and Hersham, Millwall and Scarborough to earn this fourth round FA Cup tie at Elland Road against a Leeds team which was standing third in the First Division, as proud as the Peacocks which provide their nickname. But Palace's manager at this time was Malcolm Allison, and if ever a match was tailor-made for the charismatic Allison to spring a shock result on behalf of an underdog, this one was it. In fact, so superb were Allison's Eagles on this day that not only were Leeds outplayed on their own pitch, but it is possible in retrospect to see that it was at this stage of Malcolm's management tenure at Selhurst Park that his side was at its peak. Admittedly, subsequent victories at Chelsea and Sunderland were equally sensational and took Palace close to their first ever appearance in an FA Cup semi-final. However, both those opponents were 'only' Second Division sides, whereas Leeds were certainly among the top sides in the country. Their team was packed with internationals, they were the FA Cup favourites and were regarded as certainties for victory on this cold January afternoon.

In the event, Leeds were completely bemused tactically by Palace's sweeper system in which Stewart Jump played as the extra man at the back and Leeds' danger men were closely marked by Palace's other outstanding defenders. The outcome of a single-goal Palace victory might mislead modern readers because in reality a four-goal margin would not have flattered the Palace this day and but for Leeds' Scottish international goalkeeper David Harvey we might have had it. But even Harvey was helpless when Palace were awarded a free kick midway through the first half, towards the left flank but in front of our fans. Peter Taylor, Palace's inspiration in this game and throughout the run to the semi-final, offered the perfect delivery and Palace's popular, powerful striker Dave Swindlehurst soared to head stylishly into the net past Harvey's right hand! Jim Cannon and captain Ian Evans were outstanding; Derek Jeffries had probably his best game for the Eagles and the youthful Nick Chatterton and Martin Hinshelwood dominated the midfield despite the presence of Billy Bremner and Terry Yorath, so that Leeds' response scarcely ever looked likely to cause the Palace any serious difficulties. When the final whistle went, the euphoria on the pitch, on the bench and among the fans did justice to what had been a champagne Palace performance.

Dave Swindlehurst turns away in triumph after his stylish header had put Palace ahead at Leeds.

Leeds United 0

Crystal Palace 1
Swindlehurst

CHELSEA v. CRYSTAL PALACE

Saturday 14 February 1976
Referee: Mr P. Partridge

FA Challenge Cup, Fifth Round
Attendance: 54,407

Because of the obvious limitations imposed by the sheer distance of Palace's third and fourth round ties at Scarborough and Leeds (and by the quarter-final at Sunderland, which was still in the future at this stage) it was the Eagles' fifth round clash at Chelsea which allowed most Palace fans to attend and so it has inevitably become the match of that fabulous FA Cup run which in retrospect epitomises the glory of it. The attendance was bigger than that attracted by the semi-final against Southampton at the same venue and most Palace fans who were at Stamford Bridge for this epic still enjoy recalling the huge swaying mass, the fighting and arrests of Chelsea's notorious North Stand morons and the unbelievable tension and passion that was generated.

But the packed stadium was precisely the setting Palace relished as they soared to new heights that afternoon (Palace had never beaten the Blues there before) and claimed the full spotlight of the London-based media. Of course, it was a situation perfectly made for manager Malcolm Allison, but it was also one at which the sheer character as well as the prodigious talent of Peter Taylor shone at their brightest. Of course, Chelsea knew how dangerous he might be and they managed to contain his threat for long periods while Taylor himself modestly admitted afterwards that he had played many better games than this one – but, ably supported by everyone of his team-mates, when it mattered, Peter was the game's outstanding star.

After half an hour of inconclusive probing by both sides, Palace – in a new, all white strip with a red and blue diagonal sash, which was to become perhaps the club's most popular strip of all time and has recently been resurrected, partly in token recognition – struck twice in three minutes. Peter Taylor beat two Blues defenders and then whacked a shot against the crossbar for Nick Chatterton, who had begun the move, to convert from close range, and then Taylor himself sent a left-footed drive past the flailing hand of Peter Bonetti.

Chelsea responded in the third quarter of the game with goals from their teenage skipper Ray Wilkins, and Steve Wicks (both of whom subsequently came to play for the Palace!), so that the

initiative now lay with the home side, but then Bill Garner recklessly fouled Alan Whittle twenty yards out from goal. Dave Swindlehurst shaped to take it but ran over the ball and Peter Taylor delicately, artistically, chipped it exquisitely over the advanced Bonetti and into the roof of the net for a simply brilliant winning goal.

Peter Taylor nets Palace's second goal at Chelsea in the fifth round.

Chelsea 2
R. Wilkins
Wicks

Crystal Palace 3
P. Taylor (2)
Chatterton

Saturday 6 March 1976
Referee: unknown

FA Challenge Cup, Sixth Round
Attendance: 53,850

Alan Whittle crashes home the goal that defeated Sunderland at Roker Park and put Palace in the FA Cup semi-final for the first time.

After two consecutive relegations and the 1974/75 season in the Third Division rarely looking as if Palace could reach the promotion places, 1975/76 promised to be much better…initially, at least! Before Christmas, Palace were well-nigh invincible in the League, appearing to be certainties for progress back to the upper divisions again, and, to begin with at least, a welcome if long overdue FA Cup run seemed unlikely to affect that outcome.

But now, after superb wins at Leeds and Chelsea had brought Malcolm Allison's Eagles to the attention of football fans throughout the country, we were one step away from a first-ever semi-final in that competition and there was no doubt that in the minds and hearts of most players, supporters, directors and the manager alike, the knock-out competition had taken precedence. By the time of this sixth round tie at Roker Park, there were quite simply no opponents in the land whom Palace feared and the club took an amazing number of fans to Wearside for a contest against the best team – and champions elect – of the Second Division, although many of them missed the first half hour because delays on the railways meant that the special trains were late in arriving (no surprise there then!)

Even if the victories over Leeds and Chelsea were brilliant, this one surpassed them. Seventeen previous visitors to Roker Park had retired unsuccessfully that season and the north-eastern cauldron had exposed several of them as unworthy opponents, but Palace were so disciplined and professional that once they had demonstrated to the Wearside players and their fans in the capacity crowd that they were neither overawed or lacking the required ability, everyone realised that a Palace victory was a distinct possibility.

Peter Wall played his best-ever game for Palace as sweeper on this afternoon, but the whole defence was in excellent, composed form, particularly in the first half when Sunderland, with the benefit of a fierce wind at their backs, dominated matters, but the balance of play became more even after the break. The crucial moment came fourteen minutes from time when Palace's inspirational Peter Taylor received a throw-out from 'keeper Paul Hammond ten yards inside his own half. He sped away, coasted past the challenges of Joe Bolton and Bobby Moncur, then cut over a cross from the by-line which Alan Whittle met in glorious style, bringing the ball under control with his right boot then swivelling and cracking it into the net.

Palace might have had another goal or two to emphasise the moral extent of the victory, but there was absolutely no question in the last quarter of an hour who had won the day, so that, even if many Palace fans has missed the start, we left the home team and fans in no doubt that we were there at the glorious finale!

Sunderland 0

Crystal Palace 1
Whittle

CRYSTAL PALACE v. BRIGHTON & HOVE ALBION (at Stamford Bridge)

Monday 6 December 1976
Referee: Mr R. Challis

FA Challenge Cup, First Round, Second Replay
Attendance: 14,118

Phil Holder in action during the initial match in the Palace-Brighton cup tie saga at Goldstone Road.

After Palace's fabulous FA Cup run to the semi-finals in 1975/76 their achievements in that competition the following season were rather more mundane. However, there was one particular match which stands forever in the memories of those (relatively few) Palace fans who braved the elements to see it.

The first round draw pitted Palace against fellow Third Division opponents Brighton. Palace were now managed by Terry Venables; Albion by Terry's former Tottenham colleague Alan Mullery, but there was certainly none of the rivalry between the clubs at the time such as exists today, though events were beginning to conspire to bring it about. Nearly 30,000 fans packed into Albion's headquarters where Rachid Harkouk notched a late equaliser to bring about a Selhurst Park replay. Rachid hit Palace's goal in that one too, but the 1-1 outcome necessitated another rematch and it took place thirteen days later at Stamford Bridge in dreadful weather which kept the attendance down to barely half the crowds that had seen the previous two games.

Palace's goal came early, before the sodden pitch became badly cut up, with strikers Steve Perrin and Dave Swindlehurst enabling Phil Holder to fire a long shot which Peter Grummitt fumbled on its way into the net. Brighton responded positively and had the initiative in the last half hour but the match is remembered for two late incidents which determined the ultimate outcome. Both drove poor Alan Mullery to fury. First, a Brighton equaliser was denied in the 74th minute when the referee awarded Palace a free kick for an obscure reason, and then, three minutes later, Barry Silkman conceded a penalty by bringing down Chris Cattlin. Brian Horton put the kick away...only for a retake to be ordered, apparently for encroachment. Horton's second effort, to the other corner, was parried by Paul Hammond and Kenny Sansom completed the Palace escape.

Albion were livid. Their manager expressed himself in vehement terms at the close to the official and then responded to the goading of the Palace fans by offering them a V-sign before disappearing from view down the tunnel to a hubbub of whistles and cat-calls.

Palace's reward was a second round tie at the end of the week against Enfield and they progressed from that to a 0-0 draw at Liverpool before going out 3-2 to the Reds in the Selhurst Park replay. But if modern Palace fans want to know where the intense feelings we all have towards the Seagulls and their followers originated, they should look no further than a wet night on a neutral ground in west London back in 1976.

Crystal Palace 1
Holder

Brighton & Hove Albion 0

Wednesday 11 May 1977   Football League, Third Division
Referee: Mr P. Reeves   Attendance: 18,451

Terry Venables had become Palace's manager on 1 June 1976 and he ushered in an era of steady, positive hardwork in fashioning a team that could battle its way out of the Third Division with some measure of skill and style, and then another one, largely from the aspiring stars of the brilliantly successful Palace Youth side, which would win the club a return to the highest level. The current article tells how the former objective was realised: the next one is the culmination of it all two years on.

The extraordinary feature of Palace's 1976/77 promotion campaign was that the Eagles never actually moved into the promotion bracket until after the final match of the season. That said, such an outcome had looked highly unlikely for long periods of the term – for example, in the first two months of the season Palace called upon no fewer than twenty different players while remaining firmly rooted in mid-table. However, by the end of April they were fourth, but still four points adrift of Wrexham in third place. Palace beat the Welshmen at Selhurst Park in their penultimate home game and were within two points of them when they travelled to The Racecourse for the final game, upon which now everything would depend.

But Palace knew that they would be without the experienced George Graham who was suspended for the vital fixture and, perhaps crucially, goalkeeper Tony Burns was injured, so twenty-year-old Peter Caswell was brought in for his debut! Although he was patently and understandably nervous (and his kicking was initially greatly affected), Peter produced a creditable performance in such a high-profile first game and he made several important saves.

Palace had enormous support for a midweek game at such a distant venue, but the side was largely on the defensive in the first quarter of the match before they took the lead. Kenny

One of Palace's goalscorers at Wrexham, Rachid Harkouk (right).

Wrexham 2
G. Whittle
Lyons

Crystal Palace 4
Swindlehurst, Perrin
Harkouk, Bourne

Wrexham v. Crystal Palace

Jeff Bourne (right).

Sansom possessed a hugely powerful long throw and he used it to great effect that evening. In the 27th minute, he sent the ball downfield to Nick Chatterton, whose low drive ricocheted off a defender's heel to Dave Swindlehurst, who forced it home from close range. Five minutes after half time they made it 2-0 and again the young left-back was the instigator. He made a fine run down the left flank, sent Barry Silkman clear and then ran towards the Wrexham goal for the cross, to put in a header that spun to Steve Perrin, who despatched it with admirable aplomb.

But now Wrexham were desperate – and dangerous. So close were the respective clubs' goal differences that a Palace win by two goals would require Wrexham to win their outstanding game, so they rallied, and to their credit surged back with two quick replies that would have made their Saturday fixture a formality. Palace's chance seemed to have gone as the minutes ticked away. I noted at the time that, as the end of the match approached, it was like a funeral among our supporters – but, with just ninety seconds remaining, it turned into a carnival in a sensational finale.

Palace had a throw-in, over in the far right-hand corner of Wrexham's half. Urged on by the Palace bench, Kenny Sansom ran over to hurl in the ball that changed the game, the result and the two clubs' destinies. In the ensuing mêlée Rachid Harkouk, on as substitute for the tiring Barry Silkman, hooked the ball home with precise accuracy, just under the bar and above the groping fingers of goalkeeper Barry Lloyd. Wrexham were stunned – and Palace came again! Harkouk slipped a perfect pass through to Jeff Bourne and the number 9 rammed it into the corner of the net for 4-2. There was barely time for Wrexham to kick-off before the final whistle and there was great jubilation on the pitch and wherever Palace people were gathered around the ground.

Palace were now in third place, one point above Wrexham, but because of the two-goal margin, Palace had a superior goal difference, so the Welsh club now had the task of beating championship contenders Mansfield at The Racecourse three days later in order to join the Stags and Brighton in the Second Division. But they were shattered men: true, they hit the post and had fervent support but, in the dying minutes, Mansfield scored a winner to conclude proceedings. A bunch of Palace fans had returned to Wrexham for the match and I don't believe any of us have ever cheered a goal for another club so loudly or for so long!

Wrexham: Lloyd, Evans, Dwyer, Davis, Roberts, Thomas, Shinton, Sutton, Ashcroft, Whittle, Lyons.
Crystal Palace: Caswell, P. Hinshelwood, Sansom, Holder, Cannon, Evans, Chatterton, Swindlehurst, Bourne, Perrin, Silkman (sub Harkouk 56).

CRYSTAL PALACE v. BURNLEY

Friday 11 May 1979
Referee: Mr A. Gunn

Football League, Second Division
Attendance: 51,482 (Selhurst record)

If Palace's promotion success of 1976/77, as epitomised by the victory recorded on the immediately preceding pages, was based – eventually – upon freescoring front men, the much more significant triumph of 1978/79 was built upon a brilliant defence. It has always been recognised that Terry Venables' Palace defence of 1978/79 has been at least equal of any the club has had, even in the top flight. Certainly it was hugely impressive. Opposing sides knew that, if the Palace scored, it was most unlikely that they would be able to reply; only on three occasions did a club score more than once against us, goalkeeper John Burridge kept a fabulous 21 clean sheets and the defensive record of conceding only 24 goals all season is Palace's best-ever, by a distance.

Again, unlike 1976/77, the Eagles spent virtually all of the 1978/79 season within the promotion places with over a third of it in the top spot and that proportion would probably have been greater but for the postponement of a mid-March home game. Thus, Palace approached the final week of the season in fourth place, on goal-difference only behind Cardiff and a point adrift of Stoke and Brighton, but still with that postponed game to be played in addition to the original last day fixtures. Palace's was at (Leyton) Orient, where two of the most popular men to play for the Palace were in the opposition line-up – goalkeeper John Jackson and the clever little goalpoacher Alan Whittle. Palace won it with a header from leading scorer Dave Swindlehurst from a Kenny Sansom cross midway through the second half.

So, the final game, the rearranged one against Burnley, held Palace's destiny. The other promotion contenders had finished their programmes and the issues were clear; a first ever victory over the Clarets would see Palace promoted as champions, although a draw would still take them up; a defeat would spell disaster.

Left-back Kenny Sansom was
outstanding in Palace's defence.

Crystal Palace 2
Walsh
Swindlehurst

Burnley 0

69

CRYSTAL PALACE v. BURNLEY

Dave Swindlehurst also excelled.

The match took place on the Friday evening prior to the FA Cup Final and it drew a crowd of staggering proportions to Selhurst Park, 51,482, obviously never to be surpassed here. The gates were closed a full hour before kick-off, there were scenes redolent of the first Wembley Cup Final as fans found unofficial means of entry and the atmosphere fairly sizzled with tension long before the start.

Burnley proved no mean opponents, resisting intense Palace pressure, perhaps somewhat fortuitously at times, for 77 minutes. Alan Stevenson made a string of fine saves, beginning in the third minute, when he collected a cheeky lob from Vince Hilaire; Jim Cannon scraped the bar and there was a profusion of other near-misses. With Palace failing to score, Burnley themselves began to threaten, led by the experienced Welsh international Leighton James and Steve Kindon and a shot from the former was headed off the line by Kenny Samsom.

But with twelve minutes left, Vince Hilaire delivered a perfect cross for young Ian Walsh to rise above his marker and head the ball like an arrow for the top corner of the net. It was a goal fit to win a championship and the pitch was immediately invaded by delighted, excited fans. Order was restored, the match proceeded and it seemed as if victory would be secured by this narrow margin, but with two minutes remaining and the great crowd heaving and swaying ecstatically in a manner which would given modern-day police and safety officers apoplexy, that game trier Dave Swindlehurst clinched the title with a right-footed drive to a roaring crescendo of sound.

The scenes at the final whistle were quite amazing. The players fled to the sanctuary of the tunnel as 20,000 fans poured onto the pitch: it was pandemonium. The seething mass of fans was good-natured, yet, in the supercharged atmosphere, there was an underlying anxiety about what might possibly happen. To the delight of the huge throng, Jim Cannon led his men up to the directors' box to receive and acknowledge the riotous cheers of their admirers – and rightly so! Palace were back in the top flight; going up as champions, there was every reason to celebrate and it was jubilation at Selhurst Park!

Crystal Palace: Burridge, P. Hinshelwood, Sansom, Kember, Cannon, Gilbert, Nicholas, Murphy, Swindlehurst, Walsh, Hilaire.
Burnley: Stevenson, Scott, Brennan, Noble, Thomson, Rodaway, Hall, Ingram, Morley, Kindon, James.

CRYSTAL PALACE v. IPSWICH TOWN

Saturday 29 September 1979
Referee: Mr T. Glasson

Football League, First Division
Attendance: 29,885

Frankly, the half decade between 1979 and 1984 was to develop into an extremely painful one for everybody connected with Crystal Palace FC, but it began in magnificent fashion and, as this particular article brilliantly demonstrates, with no hint of the traumas that were to follow.

Palace made two major signings in the aftermath of promotion, each of which raised the level of our record transfer fee. First to arrive was former England skipper Gerry Francis who cost us £465,000 from Queens Park Rangers, then came England B international striker Mike Flanagan for £650,000 from Charlton.

Thus augmented, Palace's first season back among the elite began in extremely encouraging fashion and as the end of September approached, Palace were lying second in the table after three wins and four draws. Their fourth top flight encounter at Selhurst Park was against Ipswich Town, managed by Bobby Robson and by now an established First Division outfit after eleven seasons there; FA Cup winners the previous year and veterans of several European campaigns. But Palace had dismissed the feeble, bad-tempered challenge of Derby County by 4-0 and that of Aston Villa 2-0 in their previous two League games at their headquarters and fans knew that, even if the Palace were regarded as underdogs, they would certainly make the Suffolk club realise that there was a new force in English football's senior division this season.

The occasion matched the glorious weather and by the finish poor Ipswich had been played off the park! In fact, Palace's first half display was absolutely outstanding. Palace fans were purring with pleasure as their youthful favourites demonstrated their talent and superiority with what was quite simply one of the best sustained spells of attacking football the club has ever produced, then emphasised it with three goals before Ipswich gained a little credibility just as the interval approached.

Dave Swindlehurst's flying volley opened the scoring against Ipswich.

Crystal Palace 4
Swindlehurst, P. Hinshelwood
Francis (pen), Cannon

Ipswich Town 1
Gates

CRYSTAL PALACE v. IPSWICH TOWN

Paul Hinshelwood celebrates his headed goal.

But the Town had no answer to Palace's inspired opening. Dave Swindlehurst rifled Palace's opening goal from a Vince Hilaire cross in the seventeenth minute, then Paul Hinshelwood headed in from a Gerry Francis free kick near the half hour. The match was over as a contest shortly afterwards: Swindlehurst burst through the middle but was clumsily halted by Russell Osman. The inevitable penalty was taken by Gerry Francis, but, with the one weak moment of the entire Palace performance, he lifted the ball over the bar...only to receive another opportunity because goalkeeper Paul Cooper moved too soon. This time Francis drilled the ball low into the net.

Yet, for all the near perfection of the Eagles' first half display, most fans who were present best recall the single goal of the second half, scored by Palace skipper Jim Cannon right on the hour. In three moves the ball travelled the entire length of the field. Vince Hilaire broke up a poor Ipswich corner and found Mike Flanagan drifting free down the left. Cannon spotted the opening and began an eighty-yard run down the middle. Flanagan saw Cannon's burst and delivered a long, dropping cross that the skipper met with an angled volley into the left-hand side of the goal netting. It brought everyone to their feet, including manager Terry Venables from the bench, who raised two clenched fists to the heavens in salute and, though no one knew it at that precise time, Jim's strike was the goal which put Palace on the top of the entire Football League. Although such was Palace's dominance for the rest of this match that the scoreline could readily have been extended at least twice and perhaps four times.

Regrettably of course, such brilliance was all too short-lived and Palace slipped from the heights, particularly after Christmas, and the club finished 1979/80 in mid-table, but those Eagles fans who were privileged to be present at Selhurst Park on this lovely autumn Saturday of 1979 treasure the memory of a unique Palace occasion. Equally, since it may be some time still before it is repeated and to confirm the matter to the club's younger or more recently secured supporters, here's how the top three places of the First Division table looked on the evening after this fabulous Palace victory:

	P	W	D	L	F	A	Pts
CRYSTAL PALACE	8	4	4	0	14	4	12
Manchester United	8	5	2	1	14	5	12
Nottingham Forest	8	5	2	1	14	6	12

Crystal Palace: Burridge, P. Hinshelwood, Sansom, Nicholas, Cannon, Gilbert, Murphy, Francis, Swindlehurst, Flanagan, Hilaire.
Ipswich Town: Cooper, Burley, Mills (sub Osborne 46), Thijssen, Osman, Butcher, Wark, Muhren, Mariner, Gates, McCall.

CRYSTAL PALACE v. BURNLEY

Tuesday 17 May 1983
Referee: Mr D. Axcell

Football League, Second Division
Attendance: 22,714

It is a bleak indication of the depths to which Palace had sunk, and how swiftly they had done so, that so soon after the splendours of the previous two articles in this book the club were in real danger of dropping out of the Second Division.

By this time Crystal Palace FC had a new owner in Ron Noades, while the current manager was Alan Mullery, a previously distinguished international player and then a successful manager with Brighton. However, Alan's two seasons at Selhurst Park were bitterly disappointing ones and 1982/83 ended with the side needing to salvage at least a draw from our final match of the term, against – of all people – Burnley. Only four years (and four pages!) previously, Palace had beaten them to win the Second Division Championship. This evening, one or the other club would be relegated. 'How are the mighty fallen' indeed!

A quite magnificent turn out by Palace fans produced an attendance that was several times greater than the average gate for the season – the biggest, in fact, since the Boxing Day visit of Arsenal in 1980! - and although there was frankly little enough for them to enthuse over during the turgid proceedings, the sheer number was an indication of the seriousness of the situation to many thousands of local people.

For long periods it appeared as if the scrappy affair would end goal-less. Burnley were neat and clever, but completely ineffective. They only managed to muster one shot of any note and that came from their substitute late on when the game was already lost and won. Credit for that fact must go to Palace's back four in particular, but Palace also found it hard to open their account, although Vince Hilaire nearly found a way through early in the second half when his shot hit the post and was cleared.

The vital moments that secured Palace's Second Division future came just after the hour when Jerry Murphy's pass enabled Henry Hughton to speed away down the right flank. From his cross, Welsh striker Ian Edwards converted a far post header. Relief flooded through every Palace person present; Burnley found themselves unable to respond at all; the Eagles grew in confidence but could add nothing to the scoreline and at the final whistle the slender victory took Palace up to fifteenth place and to survival. The fans swarmed on to the pitch in droves; champagne flowed in the dressing room – but it was to be a long while before the Eagles could truly be said to have soared again.

Kevin Mabbutt watches this effort beat the Burnley defence but finish wide of the visitors' goal.

Crystal Palace 1
Edwards

Burnley 0

CRYSTAL PALACE v. PORTSMOUTH

Saturday 20 April 1985   Football League, Second Division
Referee: Mr D. Brazier   Attendance: 10,215

It had been a trying and demanding season for Crystal Palace FC and its fans so that when the Eagles viewed their final six matches there was still a shadow of possible relegation. With only one win in the last seven games, and two in the last twelve, it is easy to see why Palace were not contemplating the last three weeks of the term with unbounded confidence, particularly since this fixture was against a promotion-chasing club, whereas the Palace were smarting from two heavy away defeats, at Leeds (1-4) and Birmingham (0-3).

The match against Pompey was as an attractive one and drew the best League crowd of the season to Selhurst Park, partly no doubt because the highly placed visitors' regular line-up included Palace's former favourites, central defender Billy Gilbert and mercurial Vince Hilaire, and many fans were eager to see how Steve Coppell's Eagles would fare against two such distinguished performers. However, the Palace boss had recently added some proven experience of his own to the side in the form of midfielder Kevin 'Ticker' Taylor and the huge former Chelsea central defender Mickey Droy. Both played a full part in Palace's success this afternoon and in the season's run-in.

Frankly, Palace exposed Portsmouth's top flight aspirations, although the Fratton Park outfit lacked three men due to suspensions, but Droy and Jim Cannon allowed them few openings; Kevin Taylor was the best midfield player on parade and Trevor Aylott bustled around effectively, causing discomfort to Pompey all the time. The match itself turned in Palace's favour as early as the eighth minute, when following an accurate Jerry Murphy free kick Mickey Droy put in a bullet header that was blocked, but then slammed in the rebound.

Vince Hilaire had a largely quiet game, but he was involved in Pompey's equaliser ten minutes later when Neil Webb picked his spot at leisure, then Andy Gray and Trevor Aylott

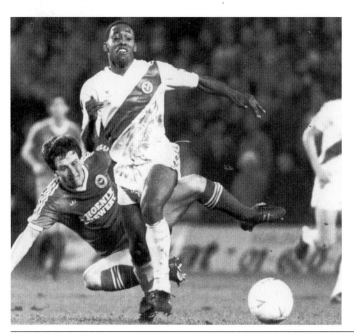

forced the agile Alan Knight to make fine saves. The second half was played at a furious pace and the fans loved every minute of it, but it was Palace who had the edge and who gained the victory they deserved with a quarter of an hour remaining, when Mickey Droy backheaded a Jerry Murphy corner and Andy Gray was able to net his fifth goal of the season from close range.

Andy Gray.

Crystal Palace 2	Portsmouth 1
Droy	*Webb*
Gray	

Tuesday 23 April 1985
Referee: Mr G. Alpin

Football League, Second Division
Attendance: 9,725

Alan Irvine.

Three days after the first-class success over Portsmouth, Palace faced an even more demanding task, for they had to travel up to industrial Lancashire to fulfil a rearranged fixture against Blackburn Rovers. Rovers had been promotion favourites all season, justifying that tag for most of it, and they were now placed in third position.

Steve Coppell naturally relied upon the same team as against Portsmouth and there was unquestionably a new-found aura of confidence about the players. Palace contained their high-flying hosts throughout the first half with a patient and disciplined display and continued to perform well after the break. Again Jim Cannon and Mickey Droy were outstanding, dealing competently with a stream of crosses from Ian Miller on Blackburn's right wing so that in this respect Blackburn played into our hands. Brian Sparrow battled hard to contain Miller, but the threat was minimised when Jerry Murphy took it upon himself to assist in that task as the match progressed.

The key moment of the game arrived just before the hour, when Palace gained a rare corner out on the right, Mickey Droy rose at the near post to flick on Jerry Murphy's kick and Alan Irvine was unchallenged at the far post to nod home and put us ahead! For obvious reasons Palace did not have many fans at Ewood Park that evening, but those who were there will never forget that moment. The goal had been scored at the 'other' end, in front of the home supporters and an eerie silence immediately descended upon the stadium – which was broken only by the hoarse yet jubilant cries of the cavorting Palace faithful behind George Wood's goal as the real-isation dawned that Palace had scored!

There followed the predictable Blackburn onslaught but, although George continued to be the busier goalkeeper, Palace were not seriously troubled in the last half hour, as they matched Rovers tackle for tackle in a full-blooded encounter that produced what was probably the club's best single result of the entire 1984/85 campaign – and in their 2,500th Football League match too!

There was one further reason for celebration: Jim Cannon made his 443rd League appear-ance that evening and thus eclipsed Terry Long's total to become Palace's foremost player in that, as in every other, competition.

Blackburn Rovers 0	Crystal Palace 1
	Irvine

Shrewsbury Town v. Crystal Palace

Sunday 18 August 1985
Referee: Mr A. Seville

Football League, Second Division
Attendance: 4,293

Phil Barber.

The Eagles' 1985/86 Football League season began twenty-four hours later than it did for everyone else (except, of course, for Shrewsbury!) because it had been necessary to delay their opening match at the Gay Meadow due to the annual flower show in the attractive Shropshire town.

The match at Shrewsbury may have been held over, but there was no holding Palace back, particularly in the first half when they were in immediate and full control. Jim Cannon and Mickey Droy were at their most resolute and George Wood exuded confidence when the side were put under pressure. Meanwhile Palace, in an all-red strip with the distinctive sash, were posing considerable problems for Shrewsbury's defence in the rain which had been falling from the start, so that it was really no surprise but most thoroughly deserved when Mickey Droy earned a throw-in deep inside home territory in the 21st minute. Palace had 'discovered' Andy Gray's long throw in the pre-season build up and it reaped its first dividend here as Mickey caused enough confusion in Shrewsbury's goal-area when it came over that there was time and space for Phil Barber to crash the ball into the net.

Having survived Shrewsbury's urgent response, Palace doubled their advantage a minute before the break when Alan Irvine's flighted corner found Andy Gray, who swivelled to score from close range.

Shrewsbury's Darren Hughes hit a post in the second half, but Palace were only denied a further goal themselves when Steve Perks saved wonderfully well from a Mickey Droy header, then Phil Barber shot wide and Andy Gray just failed to reach an inviting cross from Alan Irvine. Understandably then, with the rain beginning to ease, Palace's fans were in jubilant mood and it was here at the Gay Meadow that they were heard to be singing Steve Coppell's name for the first time, during the closing stages of the game.

Shrewsbury Town 0

Crystal Palace 2
Barber
Gray

CRYSTAL PALACE v. OLDHAM ATHLETIC

Saturday 12 October 1985
Referee: Mr R. Hamer

Football League, Second Division
Attendance: 5,243

This match provided the occasion when Ian Wright first put his name on a Football League scoresheet and turned a game with his mercurial brilliance.

There was no shortage of incident in the first 86 minutes of the game, in which Oldham took an early lead when John Ryan's cross from the right was chested down and stabbed past George Wood by Roger Palmer with Palace's defence all at sea, but eight minutes before the half-time interval the visitors failed to clear a Kevin Taylor free-kick and Alan Irvine rasped home a low drive from fifteen yards. Oldham regained the lead on the stroke of half time when David Fairclough, the original Liverpool 'super-sub', cut in from the left to score with an angled drive. Meanwhile, a stunning Mickey Droy volley had been disallowed for offside by Phil Barber and Mickey was only deprived later by an extremely vigilant referee, who ruled that a header from the huge defender had been hooked away by a relieved John Ryan without crossing the line.

The eventual outcome hinged upon the substitution of Trevor Aylott by Ian Wright with twenty minutes left, but the afternoon's activities will always be remembered for the final four minutes as Oldham desperately sought to protect their lead. It was then that Jim Cannon combined with fellow Scot Alan Irvine to set up Kevin Taylor for a neat equaliser and this was followed by Ian Wright's winner mere seconds from the final whistle. His exuberance and pace had already troubled Oldham following his 70th-minute appearance as our substitute, but when Alan Irvine floated over a tanta-lising cross, he leapt high, above and beyond the somewhat statuesque, tiring defenders, and headed past Andy Goram to turn Palace's despair into complete ecstasy.

An analytical approach would probably have made Alan Irvine Palace's man of the match – he had been involved in all three goals – but because of the dramatic finale, the afternoon will always be remembered as belonging to Ian Wright.

Kevin Taylor.

Crystal Palace 3	Oldham Athletic 2
Irvine, Taylor	*Palmer*
Wright	*Fairclough*

CRYSTAL PALACE v. IPSWICH TOWN

Saturday 15 November 1986

Football League, Second Division

Referee: Mr J.E. Gray

Attendance: 7,138

A dreadful run of five consecutive defeats in October and early November 1986 saw the Eagles slip from the top of the Second Division and hastened the signing of a player who was to become one of the greatest ever to don a Palace shirt – Mark Bright.

Mark's Palace debut was against powerful Ipswich Town, who had been relegated from the top flight some six months earlier but were now lying several places ahead of the Eagles and were among the favourites for an immediate return. Thus, all but the final minute of the first half was anything but a happy one for the new striker or for Palace's loyal fans because Ipswich dominated the proceedings, forging a two-goal lead with apparently no great effort, both their goals coming from Kevin Wilson.

However, Palace's fightback began just as the interval approached and was inspired by their new star. A Gary Stebbing cross was headed on by Ian Wright and Mark Bright, reacting commendably quickly for a man just out of reserve team football, shot on the turn, the ball entering the net past the startled goalkeeper off the back of big defender Ian Cranson.

Palace played as men transformed in the second half with Bright now excelling as a target man. Paul Cooper saved well from a Steve Ketteridge screamer, then from a delicate Kevin Taylor chip, while Atkins scraped a Bright header off the line. Then, suddenly, the experienced visitors pounced again and with just sixteen minutes left appeared to have won the contest with Wilson's third goal. Probably a season or two before Palace would have surrendered – but not this time!

Inside a minute Kevin Taylor unleashed a thirty-yard rocket that beat Cooper and went in off the bar: Ketteridge hit a post, Cooper saved well from Bright. Then, in injury time, Anton Otulakowski earned a corner, took it himself and Gavin Nebbeling headed down for Ian Wright to steer home for the draw which was the least that we deserved for our second-half efforts. That said, the inspiration for the revival had been down to one man's efforts – new boy Mark Bright.

Mark Bright.

Crystal Palace 3
Bright, Taylor
Wright

Ipswich Town 3
K. Wilson (3)

Saturday 2 January 1988
Referee: Mr P. Tyldesley

Football League, Second Division
Attendance: 10,104

George Wood.

An exciting eight-goal thriller proved wonderful entertainment for the fans of both clubs, but in retrospect this was a sad occasion for Palace folk because an horrendous blunder by George Wood epitomised the fact that this must be his last League appearance for Palace, after serving with distinction since joining us from Arsenal in the summer of 1983.

Palace fans of the period look back to this game as the one where George signed his own departure notice. The error came about when Palace were leading 4-2, ten minutes into the second half. George advanced from his area towards the right touchline to clear a loose ball. He could, and should, have walloped it to safety, but instead elected to side-foot it up the line … straight to Leicester's Paul Reid, who collected it then drove it straight into Palace's untenanted goal from more than 40 yards. The Filberts gained hope of a reprieve as a result and Mike Newell added to George's embarrassment a little later, rounding him to provide a simple tap-in for Steve Wilkinson to equalise.

Phil Barber had put away a Glenn Pennyfather cross as the quarter hour approached but Steve Brien converted a Gary McAllister cross to equalise, only for the little former Southend star to restore Palace's lead with a 25-yard drive. Leicester responded with a McAllister penalty but Palace upped the tempo and appeared to have matters firmly under control by half time. First Jim Cannon pressurised Phil Horner into a poor clearance which Ian Wright was able to loop over the goalkeeper with a header, then Ian volleyed another after Neil Redfearn's cross had been nodded back for him by ever-improving Alan Pardew.

Let's allow Steve Coppell the final word on both the game and his goalkeeper. 'Of course we should never have allowed Leicester to get back into the match after being in front three times' he said. 'Wood made a big mistake but I don't like criticising him. His brilliant goal-keeping has saved us many times.' This assessment was reasoned, gracious and entirely fair, as one would expect from a man of Steve's calibre – but equally he had no other professional option than to replace George, and he did so just ten days later.

Leicester City 4
Brien, McAllister (pen)
Reid, Wilkinson

Crystal Palace 4
Barber, Pennyfather
Wright (2)

CRYSTAL PALACE v. BIRMINGHAM CITY

Saturday 13 May 1989
Referee: Mr M.J. Bodenham

Football League, Second Division
Attendance: 17,581

This picture of the 1988/89 Palace team shows most of the heroes of that promotion season.

The position at the top of the Second Division on the last day of the normal 1988/89 season, as it affected Crystal Palace, was clear…and yet confused! Palace were already assured of appearing in the play-offs, but they might, just, gain outright promotion if Manchester City lost at Bradford City, we beat Birmingham and the aggregate goal difference on the day amounted to six goals in our favour!

Thus the setting was fit for a carnival and the Eagles responded in suitable style early in the proceedings to get the party under way. In only the 11th minute John Pemberton earned a corner out on Palace's right and when the kick came over Ian Wright tucked a header into the net at the far post. But, almost immediately, and, it seemed, with pre-meditation, some hundreds of visiting supporters invaded the pitch over in the corner by the visitors' compound. They created ugly scenes, scuffling and fighting with Palace supporters and the club stewards. They were only dispelled when a posse of mounted police galloped into the arena, but the referee had had no alternative but to remove the players from the pitch and there was a delay of almost half an hour before the match could resume, but by then it was half time at Valley Parade and the Bantams were beating Manchester City by a single goal.

Palace were now rampant, romping to a 4-0 advantage within the next twenty minutes. First, Blues defender Ian Clarkson turned a centre from Mark Bright into his own net and four minutes later Ian Wright increased the lead with a header. But perhaps the best goal was the last one, when Palace had a free kick some twenty yards out: Phil Barber touched it to one side for Ian Wright to complete an 18 minute hat-trick with a thunderous shot.

Just as Palace's delayed second half started, they heard that Manchester City had equalised but they continued to pound away at the Birmingham defence, although without reward. Then, as the results came through from elsewhere, everyone learned that City had gained the point that ensured their outright promotion so that, regardless of the Selhurst Park outcome, Palace would finish third. As Steve Coppell put it, 'the final quarter of our game was a futile exercise', and so anti-climactic was it that Birmingham grabbed a single consolation goal.

Crystal Palace 4
Wright (3)
Clarkson (og)

Birmingham City 1
Sturridge

Saturday 3 June 1989   Football League, Second Division Play-Off Final
Referee: Mr G. Courtney   Attendance: 30,000   (Second leg)

This match had enormous significance for both clubs, but for Palace the task was clearcut; they had to deny Blackburn anything and score three goals themselves to win outright, or net twice and gain promotion on the away goals rule following their 3-1 defeat at Ewood Park in the first leg.

What was probably Blackburn's best chance of upsetting Palace's calculations came early when Ian Miller struck a tenth-minute effort a foot over the bar from the edge of the penalty area, but Palace quickly moved into top gear themselves and making a telling contribution. In the 16th minute tenacious work by David Burke and Phil Barber sent Alan Pardew away down the Palace left wing. There followed an exquisite few seconds as Alan crossed accurately with the outside of his right boot, finding Ian Wright marauding close to the Rovers' goal. Terry Gennoe kept out but could not hold Ian's first effort and, amid much confusion, Ian tucked the ball away at the second attempt.

The fans exploded with delight and Palace attacked remorselessly, if unsuccessfully, for the rest of the first half amid unbelievable tension. But that pressure took its toll on Blackburn and the visitors' hopes of keeping their opponents at bay soon evaporated in the second half. Their defence was in such disarray under the storming raids that in the 47th minute it snapped. Eddie McGoldrick made a run, cut in along the edge of the penalty area and was bundled over by Mark Atkins as he played the ball away. Referee George Courtney signalled 'penalty'. It was a debatable decision but he had been perfectly placed to see what had happened and it was nowhere near as contentious as the award given in Blackburn's favour which had turned the League match between the clubs at Ewood Park during the previous autumn.

Dave Madden took control, stepped up and coolly slotted home the award, low, to the goal-keeper's left side and into the Whitehorse Lane goal. Palace continued as the aggressors but were unable to break through again and in the last twenty minutes Blackburn began to assert themselves more, because of course a goal for them would virtually have ended the affair. But the Eagles' defence held firm, with Gary O'Reilly outstanding and Perry Suckling bringing off one fabulous save, so that ninety minutes were reached with the sides still locked together at an aggregate scoreline of three goals apiece.

So, to extra time and the minutes ticked away with

Ian Wright scores Palace's first goal in the play-off final against Blackburn.

Crystal Palace 3   Blackburn Rovers 0   (after extra time)
Wright (2)
Madden (pen)

CRYSTAL PALACE v. BLACKBURN ROVERS

Here's Ian Wright, again causing consternation in the Rovers ranks.

both sides going close but neither able to score. Perry Suckling tipped over a Simon Garner effort and Palace knew that they only needed to hold on to earn promotion. But then, with Blackburn stretched after pressing up in a desperate attempt to make the decisive strike, Eddie McGoldrick battled his way to the by-line under the Arthur Wait Stand and in front of the Whitehorse Lane end, and with just two minutes left, Ian Wright leapt like a salmon to head home the cross unchallenged!

Pandemonium erupted as the ecstatic crowd invaded the pitch, but the fans were quickly cleared by the police and stewards with much good humour all round. Perry Suckling held a cunning, curling effort from Scott Sellars in Rovers' last attack and then came the final whistle! The players were engulfed but finally managed to reach the tunnel and appeared in the director's box to the strains of 'Glad All Over' playing repeatedly over the public address system.

History had been made – Palace were back in the top flight and the Football League play-offs never again had a two-legged final. However, the final word on this match and the whole occasion should rest with Steve Coppell who, as ever, had it perfectly analysed: 'Play-offs are cruel' he said, 'but our performance here was nothing short of magnificent.'

Crystal Palace: Suckling, Pemberton, Burke, Madden, Hopkins, O'Reilly, McGoldrick, Pardew, Bright, Wright, Barber.
Blackburn Rovers: Gennoe, Atkins, Sulley, Reid, Hendry, Mail, Gayle (sub Ainscow 104), Millar, Miller (sub Curry 57), Garner, Sellars.

Manchester United v. Crystal Palace

Saturday 9 December 1989
Referee: Mr T. Simpson

Football League, First Division
Attendance: 33,514

Palace manager Steve Coppell had initially been most prudent in the matter of new players to strengthen Palace's promotion-winning squad, but in the early winter of 1989 he secured the country's first £1 million goalkeeper in Nigel Martyn from Bristol Rovers and former Wimbledon centre half Andy Thorn from Newcastle for £650,000. The pair lined up together for Andy's Palace debut in this testing fixture at Old Trafford and we began the game with five men at the back to accommodate him.

Palace had not profited much from their First Division travels thus far in 1989/90 (two points from seven outings), but nevertheless the fans were in Manchester in great numbers and were rewarded by a simply splendid performance which was capped by their first top-flight success of the term away from Selhurst Park. It is doubtful too if Steve Coppell can have found any Palace performance more rewarding than this one, taking place as it did on the ground he had graced with such distinction for so long.

Not that it looked like falling out that way at first because, in spite of Palace's augmented defence, we trailed as early as the ninth minute when United's Russell Beardsmore put them ahead with a diving header from a Lee Martin cross, and for a while only Nigel Martyn's brilliance prevented the Red Devils from adding to their lead. They say that goalkeepers don't win matches, but this performance from Nigel certainly made victory possible because, after he had denied United further reward for a full half an hour, Palace levelled with their first serious attack. Although Palace were playing without either of their recognised wide men at this stage of the game, it was from a move down the flank that they equalised. Ian Wright gained possession on the right, his pace was simply too much for United and he crossed from a position inside the penalty area near the by-line for Mark Bright to head powerfully past the exposed

Captains in contest! Palace skipper Geoff Thomas fends off a challenge from his United counterpart Bryan Robson.

Manchester United 1
Beardsmore

Crystal Palace 2
Bright (2)

Mark Bright crashes a header past Jim Leighton for the equaliser.

Leighton and into the top corner of the net – right in front of the Palace fans who had travelled north for the game.

There was yet more to come. Nine minutes after the break, Andy Gray swung the ball out to overlapping John Pemberton. 'Pembo's' athleticism frequently astonished seasoned top flight opponents throughout 1989-90 and on this occasion he sped to the by-line at the Stretford End then crossed for Mark Bright to head a glancing second, with the ball squirming in low, underneath the hapless 'keeper.

United of course responded, but Martyn and his colleagues defended admirably and United's finishing was all too frequently wayward, so that the nearest thing to another goal was when Mark Bright was only denied a hat-trick of headers with a quarter of an hour to go, watching in disappointment along with his team-mates as his effort from substitute Phil Barber's cross bounced off the top of United's crossbar.

Let's give Andy Thorn the last word about this memorable Palace success. Asked by a pressman after the game for his comments, Palace's new star responded 'This is a hard place to come to at any time and we had to weather the storm after United scored so early'. Andy then lifted his chin and fixed the reporter with his eye: 'But this Palace side can certainly score goals. The problem has been the number they have been conceding and hopefully I can help them do something about that.' So successful was Andy in that quest that Palace finished the season comfortably in mid-table, gaining one or two more noteworthy results along the way, and ended it with a showpiece pair of games against United at Wembley – as will shortly be revealed.

Manchester United: Leighton, Beardsmore, Martin, Bruce, Phelan (sub Blackmore 81), Pallister, Robson, Ince, McClair, Wallace, Sharpe (sub Hughes 56).
Crystal Palace: Martyn, Pemberton, Dennis, Gray (sub Barber 78), Hopkins, O'Reilly, Thorn, Thomas, Bright, Wright, Pardew.

CHARLTON ATHLETIC v. CRYSTAL PALACE

Saturday 16 December 1989
Referee: Mr G. Tyson

Football League, First Division
Attendance: 15,762

A week after Palace's stunning victory at Old Trafford, they faced another away fixture, but one that was totally unique in the club annals for it was against their tenants, Charlton, and thus, for the first time, Palace were the visiting side at their own ground. Eagles supporters were largely contained in the Arthur Wait stand and were delighted as the side earned a second 'away' victory in eight days with their recent signings Nigel Martyn and Andy Thorn displaying quite outstanding form. Indeed, with only four minutes gone, Andy rose at the far post at the Whitehorse Lane end to head a free kick from Andy Gray powerfully past Valiants' skipper Bob Bolder. The goalkeeper saved well from Ian Wright, but then Jeff Hopkins headed on an Eddie McGoldrick left-side corner in the 26th minute for Mark Bright to net at the far post in typically predatory style.

Charlton had a great opportunity to get quickly back into the match, for, shortly after the half hour, Jeff Hopkins was adjudged to have fouled the waif-like Kenny Achampong, but a rare miss from the penalty spot by their normally deadly exponent Mark Reid cost them that chance. Reid lanced his kick onto the left-side post and John Pemberton hoofed the rebound cheerfully to safety.

Charlton brought on both of their substitutes after the interval, rearranging their side somewhat and, with the wind behind them, they began to make Palace's defence look rather uneasy. When Charlton scored on the hour with a fine free kick by Colin Walsh, Palace might have buckled under the ensuing pressure. The fact that they did not was due, largely, to a fine game from Andy Gray, a demonstration by Andy Thorn that his £650,000 transfer fee could be regarded as an investment, some solid defending in all other quarters but, supremely, to Nigel Martyn, who made two superb fisted saves from Robert Lee and Paul Williams earlier in the match and produced another absolutely brilliant one to deny Micky Bennett's last-minute header from point blank range.

Of course, Palace fans have grown used to watching their teams play 'away' games at Selhurst Park since this match, but this one was the first of them and was therefore an unrepeatable occasion. The Charlton line-up was remarkable in that it contained no fewer than three men who were soon to be wearing the Eagles' colours.

Recent signing Andy Thorn was outstanding against Charlton.

Charlton Athletic 1
Walsh

Crystal Palace 2
Thorn
Bright

CRYSTAL PALACE v. LIVERPOOL (at Villa Park)

Sunday 8 April 1990
Referee: Mr G.C. Courtney

FA Challenge Cup, Semi-Final
Attendance: 38,389

For what it's worth, my guess would be that what follows will be the most popular account in this book – certainly for any early twenty-first century readers! The sheer size of Palace's task in this FA Cup semi-final was enormous. Liverpool were the FA Cup holders and the clear leaders at the top of the First Division table, looking every inch the champions-elect, while of course they had already beaten Palace 9-0 at Anfield and 2-0 at Selhurst Park. Add to the equation the facts that Palace would have to meet the northern giants without Ian Wright or Eddie McGoldrick, while proven defenders Mark Dennis, Jeff Hopkins and David Burke were all also sidelined and it is easy to see that the pundits and even many Palace fans feared that Palace's exit from the competition was at hand.

However, Steve Coppell and his men refused to go along with such gloomy prognostications. 'One-off matches are great occasions for the under-dogs' averred the Palace manager and Palace fans certainly knew that Liverpool would be surprised by their determination and staying power. Indeed, in the end, while no-one was in the least surprised by the fact that Liverpool scored three more goals against us to take their tally against the Eagles to an amazing fourteen, almost everybody was completely astounded when the Palace notched up four goals of their own. That was what completely upset the script and totally confounded the apparently all-knowing media gurus.

Not, it must be admitted, that there was really any suggestion in the somewhat dour first half that the huge and boisterous following of Palace fans at Villa Park would be present to witness such a glorious occasion, for, although we settled down quickly enough and showed little sign of nerves, Palace's difficult task was made much harder when, after only 14 minutes, their offside trap failed, allowing Ian Rush to take a superb pass from Steve McMahon and beat Nigel

Martyn for his 23rd goal of the season. It may have been significant too that, in this first period, Rush had to leave the field after 29 minutes with a bruised rib, and Palace spent the rest of the half ensuring that no further damage was sustained to their cause.

However, Palace's performance in the second half and in extra time surpassed anything that the club had ever previously produced, to destroy Liverpool. Within sixteen seconds of the restart Palace were level: John Pemberton strode away down the right flank on a sixty-yard

Geoff Thomas takes the ball past Liverpool's Gary Gillespie.

Crystal Palace 4	Liverpool 3	(after extra time)
Bright, O'Reilly	*Rush, McMahon*	
Gray, Pardew	*Barnes (pen)*	

Alan Pardew is mobbed by his delighted team-mates after scoring the winner at Villa Park.

run, then put over a cross which created panic in Liverpool's defence. Phil Barber's effort was thwarted, then John Salako's shot was blocked by substitute Steve Staunton, but the ball flew to Mark Bright on the volley and Palace's greatest goalscorer hit a shot which rocketed into the top corner of Grobbelaar's net, right in front of the jubilant Palace fans who now, like the players, sensed that the day and the match could be theirs.

Liverpool simply could not cope with Palace's sustained aerial assault and Palace, having exposed their weakness, exploited it regularly. At every opportunity they launched high balls into the danger zone and began to take control of the game, as Richard Shaw allowed Peter Beardsley no scope at all for manoeuvre and the Reds' international midfielders Ronnie Whelan and Steve McMahon found it increasingly hard to restrain the surging runs of Geoff Thomas or Alan Pardew's telling passes.

Come the 69th minute and Liverpool were facing possible defeat when an Andy Gray free kick was headed down by Phil Barber and Gary O'Reilly thumped the ball emphatically into the net from ten yards' range. But for all Palace's supreme efforts, Liverpool still possessed talent of the topmost quality and they responded inside the 81st minute with a two-goal salvo in ninety seconds to retrieve the lead, McMahon scoring with a scorching drive from the edge of the penalty area and John Barnes from the penalty spot itself, after John Pemberton was somewhat harshly adjudged to have fouled Staunton.

That double blow would have ended the challenge of most clubs but Palace set out to discover another chink in the Liverpool armour and with just two minutes of ordinary time remaining they found it. Again, Liverpool had no answer to a lofted free kick from John Pemberton and in the ensuing mêlée Andy Gray headed Palace's equaliser.

Palace might have won it there and then had an Andy Thorn header gone in instead of rocking the crossbar, but Liverpool could not take advantage of that reprieve and in the compelling extra time Palace produced the final twist to a magical afternoon. Once more Liverpool were in complete disarray following a Palace set piece early in the second period when an Andy Gray corner on the left was flicked on by Andy Thorn at the edge of the six-yard area, for Alan Pardew to head the decisive fourth goal into the net behind which were ranked Palace's now ecstatic fans.

Crystal Palace: Martyn, Pemberton, Shaw, Gray, O'Reilly, Thorn, Barber, Thomas, Bright, Salako, Pardew.
Liverpool: Grobbelaar, Hysen, Burrows, Gillespie (sub Venison 45), Whelan, Hansen, Beardsley, Houghton, Rush (sub Staunton 29), Barnes, McMahon.

CRYSTAL PALACE v. MANCHESTER CITY

Saturday 5 May 1990
Referee: Mr D. Hutchinson

Football League, First Division
Attendance: 20,056

Nigel Martyn – the country's first £1-million goalkeeper and a superb acquisition.

The 1989/90 Football League season finished with Palace at home to Manchester City, but with the FA Cup final imminent, it was inevitable that this match would be an Eagles fiesta at Selhurst Park. However, there was a surprise for the fans on this sweltering afternoon – the pitch was straw-yellow! Prolonged hot sunshine had grossly accelerated the reaction of the herbicide applied at this time every year and the effect was dramatic to say the least.

Palace refused to take the last match as a canter in the sun and, setting off at great pace, surprised City so much that Palace were two up in ten minutes! Mark Bright headed down a John Salako cross inside the penalty area for Alan Pardew to show neat control before flicking the ball past Andy Dibble, then Andy Gray blasted a ferocious free kick into the top corner – but this was where the carnival ended for the Palace and their fans.

City supporters paraded with well-wishing banners for the Cup Final at half time but what followed was certainly not one of the club's best halves of the season. No doubt some minds had already moved on to Wembley. City pulled a goal back in the 71st minute when their substitute, former Palace man Clive Allen, beat Nigel Martyn from the penalty spot with his first kick of the match after Gary O'Reilly had handled and then Palace striker Garry Thompson was dismissed for two bookable fouls.

Despite the handicap of playing with only ten men in the heat, Palace appeared to have a morale-boosting victory within their grasp, but two minutes from time City's beanpole centre forward Niall Quinn equalised, although Eagles supporters will always contend that he controlled the ball with his hand before prodding it past a bewildered Nigel Martyn.

The Palace players took their customary and richly deserved lap of honour at the end of the last home game and Palace fans then raced across the pitch to the visitors' corner, to applaud the visiting supporters whose sportsmanship and enthusiasm had contributed greatly to a particularly special afternoon's entertainment.

Crystal Palace 2
Pardew
Gray

Manchester City 2
Allen (pen)
Quinn

CRYSTAL PALACE v. MANCHESTER UNITED (at Wembley Stadium)

Saturday 12 May 1990
Referee: Mr A. Gunn

FA Challenge Cup, Final
Attendance: 80,000

The famous Twin Towers of Wembley.

Two issues exercised the minds of Palace folk as the 1990 FA Cup final approached. The first concerned Ian Wright's recovery from the twice broken leg which had kept him out of the semi-final; the second was the pressing matter of securing a ticket from the Eagles' modest allocation of little more than fourteen thousand. But if the Palace fans at Wembley were fewer in number than the followers of Manchester United, they certainly gave the team a huge boost during the preliminaries with the spectacular release of thousands of red and blue helium filled balloons just as the players entered the arena.

Heartened perhaps by this display, Palace started the game well and after little more than a quarter of an hour they were awarded a free kick out on the right. Andy Gray feinted a right-footed cross but Phil Barber delivered a left-footed curler which Gary O'Reilly reached before anyone else and his header looped off Pallister, over Leighton and into the net in front of the phalanx of Palace fans! United replied ten minutes before half time with a goal from Bryan Robson which took a wicked deflection off John Pemberton's shin.

By the interval it was apparent how Palace were shackling United's supremely talented attacking and midfield stars. We were deploying a tight, even rigid, man-to-man marking system, aimed at harassing United, denying them room, forcing them backwards or into errors and then hoping to capitalise on set pieces as we had against Liverpool in the semi-final. It had all worked sufficiently well in the opening forty-five minutes and if, through fatigue and the quality of the opposition, it did not fare quite so effectively afterwards, the second half and extra time provided compelling entertainment and will rank among Palace's best ever performances for a long, long time.

Mark Hughes put United ahead soon after the hour, but then Steve Coppell made his perfectly judged substitution, bringing on Ian Wright to replace Phil Barber after 69 minutes. Within three minutes Palace were level with a goal to match the finest the old stadium had ever seen. The lissom, eager Palace striker skipped clear of the lunging Mike Phelan, turned inside Pallister – the defender who alone at £2.3 million had cost most than our entire team! – then

---

Crystal Palace 3
O'Reilly
Wright (2)

Manchester United 3
Robson
Hughes (2)

(after extra time)

CRYSTAL PALACE v. MANCHESTER UNITED

The Eagles are ahead! Gary O'Reilly's looping header has United's defence in confusion.

delivered a low shot past Leighton for 2-2. The initiative now lay with Palace and they might have won the Cup there and then. United were uncertain – but while Palace found the goal, they did not do so until two minutes into extra time. It was another strike of the highest quality too. Young John Salako sent over a long testing cross from the left. Wright saw it first and early and volleyed the ball into the net while flying some five feet above the turf! What a Cup winner it would have been, but unfortunately United still had sufficient time to regroup and to show one more moment of high class finishing, Hughes taking advantage of a moment of tired defending to make it 3-3 and to force a replay the following Thursday.

Crystal Palace: Martyn, Pemberton, Shaw, Gray (sub Madden 117), O'Reilly, Thorn, Barber (sub Wright 69), Thomas, Bright, Salako, Pardew.
Manchester United: Leighton, Ince, Martin (sub Blackmore 88), Bruce, Phelan, Pallister (sub Robins 93), Robson, Webb, McClair, Hughes, Wallace.
Referee: Mr A. Gunn.

The replay requires some, minor, comment. It was tense dour and closely fought – and won by United on the hour. In fact, the game turned on the referee's decision to award a Palace free kick outside the penalty area (by some distance!) when the marks of the incident on the turf clearly showed that the foul on Geoff Thomas had occurred inside it.

One day, hopefully before too long, Palace will have another opportunity to contest the final for the famous trophy and this time return to Selhurst Park with it in triumph!

NORWICH CITY v. CRYSTAL PALACE

Saturday 8 September 1990
Referee: Mr K. Cooper

Football League, First Division
Attendance: 15,306

Norwich have always been a difficult side to beat on their own terrain regardless of in which competition Palace have met them, but this emphatic victory remains statistically Palace's best against them in Norfolk and was secured with a splendidly professional performance.

The opening goal came after only six minutes. A John Salako cross from the right proved too much for Bryan Gunn, who was under pressure from Garry Thompson. He flapped weakly at it, then had to watch in dismay as it fell perfectly for Phil barber to volley, unchallenged, into the net. Six minutes later an Andy Gray pass set up Geoff Thomas. The skipper's shot was blocked but the ball ran to Ian Wright, who powered home the rebound from just inside the penalty area. 'Glad All Over' echoed around Carrow Road from this point, even when Norwich were attempting to remedy their plight, and Eric Young might have added to the Canaries' discomfort when he moved upfield for a free kick, but he lifted a half chance over the bar.

Norwich substitute Ruel Fox showed some eagerness for their cause and it took one particularly fine save by Nigel Martyn to deny him, but John Salako ended any ambitions Norwich might have entertained just nine minutes into the second half. Andy Thorn struck a splendidly judged, fifty yard through ball past the City's square-lying back four and Palace's Nigeria-born winger brought the ball down with his first touch, then stroked it past Gunn with his second for a glorious goal.

Not surprisingly, Steve Coppell was moved to praise his men after the game. 'From a professional point of view, this was our best performance for a long time' said the boss, and those readers who know Steve's reputation for economy with words will realise that this represented a glowing accolade. That it was most thoroughly deserved is reinforced by the performance falling on the first anniversary of Palace's 9-0 defeat at Anfield. The Eagles were second in the First Division table and the only side above us was...Liverpool!

There was considerable interest in this League Cup tie before the game because the fixture would bring three former Palace men back to Selhurst in the persons of goalkeeper Paul Sansome, defender Chris Powell and striker Andy Ansah, but by the end of the evening the Palace crowd were in ferment since the occasion had caused the record books to be re-written after

Phil Barber congratulates Ian Wright.

Norwich City 0

Crystal Palace 3
Barber, Wright
Salako

CRYSTAL PALACE v. SOUTHEND UNITED

Tuesday 25 September 1990   Football League Cup, Second Round, First Leg
Referee: Mr G. Singh   Attendance: 9,653

the annihilation of the team from Roots Hall. Mark Bright partnered Ian Wright in a Palace starting line-up for the first time since the latter had broken his leg eight months before – and how poor Paul Sansome must have rued that statistic! It was Bright who gave Palace the lead in only the second minute when he cut down the left flank, veered towards goal, drew the 'keeper then despatched his low shot with aplomb. Southend responded with spirit and no small ability so that Palace had cause to be grateful to Ian Wright who dispossessed a defender, then, again from the left, made the most of the opening his tenacity had created.

Palace were unable to add further to the scoreline before the break but just five minutes into the second half Glyn Hodges had an easy task after Sansome had parried a piledriver from Ian Wright. Any doubts as to the outcome were settled in the 71st minute when Mark Bright turned in a cross from Wright after the latter's blistering pace had taken him clear of all defenders.

Now Steve Coppell brought on Garry Thompson as a third all-out attacker and the goal tally mounted inexorably – and at a pace only once bettered at the club. Ian Wright headed in a fifth off the crossbar following a Glyn Hodges corner, then completed his hat-trick in the 80th minute with a deflected shot after another corner. Nigel Martyn prevented a Shrimpers response when he denied Steve Tilson, then Garry Thompson converted a Hodges free kick. The final strike came three minutes from the end when Mark Bright notched his own hat-trick by glancing in a delicate header from a Geoff Thomas long throw.

Mark and Ian claimed the matchball as the sides left the field – they gave it away to a charity auction afterwards – but the best remark of the night belonged to the beleaguered Southend manager, Dave Webb: 'We'll get them in the second leg' he quipped. 'We'll turn out the lights, then they won't be able to see what we're up to!'

Ian Wright scored a hat-trick against Southend ...

... as did Mark Bright.

Crystal Palace 8   **Southend United 0**
 Bright (3), Wright (3)
 Hodges, Thompson

Saturday 27 October 1990
Referee: Mr G.R. Pooley

Football League, First Division
Attendance: 17,220

Geoff Thomas salutes his goal against Wimbledon.

The earliest stages of this match gave little hope that the Eagles might be about to secure a third consecutive victory over Wimbledon for, with only nine minutes gone, Paul McGee swivelled on the ball some thirty yards out from the goal, spotted that Nigel Martyn had strayed too far from his goal-line and floated a delightful chip over him into the net for a splendidly opportunistic goal. However, four minutes later McGee unnecessarily conceded a corner on Palace's right from which they got back on terms. John Salako played the ball low to Ian Wright on the edge of the penalty area and his left-footed cross was met perfectly by Geoff Thomas soaring high and unchecked in the middle of the goal area to score with a deliberate header.

Although there was lots of excitement and no little skill for the fans to savour, the scoreline remained unchanged until the interval, but the second half produced five goals of really high quality. Five minutes after the restart, John Salako's trickery on the right flank opened the Don's defence again for Ian Wright. Goalkeeper Hans Segars managed to block the first effort but the ball rebounded to John Humphrey, who was lurking on the edge of the penalty area, and he slid it home along the ground into the vacant net to record a rare strike in his long and distinguished career. Segers then produced a series of first-class saves but was powerless to stop Andy Gray from crashing in following a Mark Bright header, then John Fashanu lobbed the ball over Martyn with a delicacy and precision seldom seen in such a big man, to bring the score back to 3-2.

The goal glut continued. A minute later, Mark Bright restored Palace's two-goal advantage with a volleyed shot off the post from a Glyn Hodges cross, but with three minutes of the match remaining little Paul McGee jinked his way past Nigel Martyn and netted, to keep us all on tenterhooks in the dying moments.

There was added pleasure for Palace fans after this victory because it established a new best-ever start to a top-flight season for the club. With ten undefeated games (five wins and five draws), Steve Coppell's Eagles had improved upon our previous best effort at this level in 1979/80 of nine unbeaten matches which comprised four wins and five draws.

Crystal Palace 4	Wimbledon 3
Thomas, Humphrey	*McGee (2)*
Gray, Bright	*Fashanu*

CRYSTAL PALACE v. LIVERPOOL

Sunday 30 December 1990
Referee: Mr R.B. Gifford

Football League, First Division
Attendance: 26,280

Palace's last game of 1990 was at home to Liverpool. The previous spring Palace had avenged their 9-0 Anfield disaster by beating the Reds in the FA Cup semi-final and now they repeated that success, showing increased maturity and such an abundance of ability that the scoreline reflected little of the Eagles' superiority!

Liverpool's line-up deployed a sweeper in the portly personage of Danish international Jan Molby, but even so they were constantly troubled on the flanks as well as at the centre, whether the ball was on the deck or hoisted high. Accordingly, Palace dominated the first half in a manner which not even their most fervent fans could have expected and which must have astonished the huge television audience. Such pressure simply had to tell.

Tell it did, three minutes before the break, with a goal of supreme quality which ignited the Selhurst Park atmosphere, rocked the Reds and demonstrated to the watching millions just how devastating our strike force could be, even against such pedigree opponents as these. Ian Wright controlled a ball from Eric Young out by the right-corner flag, rounded Gary Gillespie then accelerated, before drilling a hard, low cross along the length of the by-line to the near post. Mark Bright was there to flash the ball past David Burrows, through Bruce Grobbelaar's legs and into the net to bring a thunderous roar of acclaim from our supporters. Selhurst Park immediately erupted to the strains of 'Glad All Over' and it was party time again at Liverpool's expense.

Naturally, Liverpool attempted to up the tempo after the interval, but Palace matched them in every respect and if Nigel Martyn now became the busier goalkeeper it was far from being one-way traffic and most referees would have awarded Palace a penalty three minutes from time when Glenn Hysen, who was inevitably beaten for pace by Ian Wright, wrestled the Palace striker to the ground, but Mr Gifford was (understandably perhaps) flagging by this late stage of a hectic afternoon and only viewed the incident from a considerable distance.

Liverpool's supremacy in the championship race faltered from this point on. Within three weeks Arsenal had taken over at the top of the table. In the final analysis Liverpool finished second with Palace third, but anyone who witnessed the match between them at the close of 1990 was left in no doubt which was the stronger of the two teams.

Mark Bright's decisive strike against Liverpool.

Crystal Palace 1	Liverpool 0
Bright	

CRYSTAL PALACE v. EVERTON (at Wembley Stadium)

Sunday 7 April 1991
Referee: Mr G. Courtney

Full Members' Cup, Final
Attendance: 52,460

Geoff Thomas climbs to his feet after heading the opening goal.

Having got so close to winning the FA Cup the previous May, Palace returned to the national stadium to claim the Full Members' Cup at the expense of Everton. No one pretended that there was a parity between the competitions, but the victory brought huge satisfaction to the Palace club and its followers.

After the teams had received a tumultuous reception in terms of colour and noise, the first half was an interesting exercise in the contrast of styles. Everton were always neat, sometimes even pretty, yet, even with a fairly attacking line-up, they showed little menace. There was also an air of tension about and perhaps it was as well that the half ended in a downpour of rain to help keep the participants' tempers off the boil, as Palace played to their proven strengths of physical fitness, direct attacks, an emphasis on set pieces and, of course, top quality finishing.

Thus, it was precisely midway through the second half that Palace forged ahead – a John Salako corner on the left was headed on by Eric Young and Geoff Thomas cleaved his way through the Toffees' static defence to net with a brave diving header. Geoff was at his peak at this stage of his career and there was no question that his inspirational leadership fully deserved the man of the match award for this game.

Everton responded almost immediately, Robert Warzycha flicking the ball past Nigel Martyn from close range. The pace of the encounter became quite tremendous and as it progressed towards the end of normal time either side might have won it, but it was during the extra thirty minutes that Palace claimed, gained and retained the ascendancy.

With four minutes to go until the extra-time interval, Palace turned the match, Ian Wright taking the pace off a huge clearance from Nigel Martyn with the sole of his boot, then turning away from a marker before beating Neville Southall with his right foot. 'Glad All Over' boomed out across the stadium from the Palace fans for it seemed unlikely that weary Everton would be able to get back on terms again now. Indeed, in the last quarter of an hour, Palace scored twice more! First, a cross by Eddie McGoldrick was touched on intelligently by Mark Bright and John Salako placed a diving header beyond the exposed Southall and just under the crossbar. Only two minutes later, Ian Wright capitalised again upon Mark Bright's selfless hard work, his pace taking him on to a header from his colleague and then sliding the ball past the now demoralised goalkeeper to secure his own second Wembley 'double'.

Crystal Palace 4	Everton 1	(after extra time)
Thomas, Wright (2)	*Warzycha*	
Salako		

CRYSTAL PALACE v. EVERTON

Wembley was a riot of red and blue balloons at the Full Members' Cup Final.

Now Palace fans simply made Wembley into the Selhurst Park of north London. They sang, cheered, shouted, waved, applauded – and some normally quite reserved folk even danced! – with delight and abandon. Their joy knew no bounds and certainly the sight of Geoff Thomas receiving the trophy will remain forever with those present. Regrettably, there was one sour note at the end when Neville Southall boycotted the presentation of medals as a one-man protest which was no credit to the fine goalkeeper or his club, but there was no doubt from Everton's attitude when they visited Selhurst Park for a League match a fortnight later that they deeply resented Palace's Wembley victory.

Crystal Palace: Martyn, Humphrey, Shaw, Gray (sub McGoldrick 54), Young (sub Thompson 116), Thorn, Salako, Thomas, Bright, Wright, Pardew.
Everton: Southall, McDonald, Hinchcliffe, Keown (sub Ratcliffe 80), Watson, Milligan, Warzycha, McCall, Newell (sub Nevin 70), Cottee, Sheedy.

Saturday 4 May 1991   Football League, First Division
Referee: Mr D. Elleray   Attendance: 10,002

Football can certainly be cruel! There's no need to state this fact to Palace fans, but the occasion now under review saw the agony piled upon our opponents. Wimbledon and their followers were coming to terms with the fact that it was necessary for their club to abandon its tight little headquarters at Plough Lane, from where they had progressed so marvellously from obscurity to top-flight status. This match was the last senior game to be staged there and what the Dons and their supporters wanted was something special to remember the old homestead by. Memorable it most certainly was, but only the Palace contingent who were present could possibly say that it brought any pleasure!

Alright, the first half was simply, stunningly, numbingly, boringly dreadful – but the second was illuminated by a hat-trick that was as brilliant as it was speedy and the man who scored it was Palace's Ian Wright. His virtuoso performance began in the 54th minute when he scored his 22nd goal of the season. Garry Thompson had headed on a long Andy Thorn free kick for Terry Phelan to nod away as far as Ian, who was steaming into the penalty area to support the attack. Without breaking stride he struck the ball low, hard and just inside the near post.

The second goal six minutes later was totally unforgettable. Steve Coppell described it as 'one of the finest pieces of individual skill I have ever seen'. The Palace striker collected Nigel Martyn's clearance just inside the Wimbledon half; he took the ball on his in-step and lifted it over Dean Blackwell on the volley, spotted that Hans Segers was off his line, then, from some forty yards, struck an audacious drifting lob over the stranded, embarrassed 'keeper, that flew into the net off an inside post. Some Palace people regard it as the best goal Ian scored for the Eagles; some say it is the best Palace goal they have ever seen. It was certainly in a class that Palace strikers have seldom emulated. Inevitably, the third goal was mundane by comparison, although it was still a quality strike. John Humprey overlapped to take a pass from John Salako and his diagonal cross was turned in at the far post by Ian Wright from a tight and ever-diminishing angle, to establish a number of club records. It was, among other things, Palace's first hat-trick on an opponent's ground since 1963, and easily their fastest at top level.

Richard Shaw shares Ian Wright's delight.

Wimbledon 0   **Crystal Palace 3**
Wright (3)

OLDHAM ATHLETIC v. CRYSTAL PALACE

Saturday 21 September 1991

Football League, First Division

Referee: Mr M.D. Reed

Attendance: 13,391

Pre-match discussions among groups of Palace fans at Boundary Park on this bright and breezy afternoon focussed mainly upon the changes forced upon the team by injuries and suspensions, among which was the further appearance of Perry Suckling in goal where he would provide another rare example of an Eagles skipper between the posts. However, what was unknown was the hugely significant fact that this would be Ian Wright's last appearance in our colours before his £2.5 million move to Arsenal, news of which broke over the weekend and which was completed some forty-eight hours later.

Playing in their attractive, new, Brazilian-style 'away' kit of yellow and blue, the Eagles were ahead within fourteen minutes. Mark Bright won the ball near the right corner flag, played a short pass to the advancing John Humphrey, then watched John Salako meet the cross with a spectacular glancing header which zipped into the bottom corner of the goal. Oldham levelled almost on the stroke of half time with two minutes of injury time already on the clock, when a defensive lapse left Ian Marshall with only Perry Suckling to beat.

But Palace were soon back in front after the restart and with a fabulous – albeit final – Ian Wright goal. Ian ran with the ball from inside the Palace half of the centre-circle for some fifty yards to the edge of the Oldham penalty area, outpacing every attempt to catch him, then

finished powerfully, clinically, left-footed and low, past the goalkeeper's right hand. It was his 117th goal from his 277 Palace appearances and a marvellous valedictory. Again Oldham responded, with the aid of a deflection, but this was to be Palace's game and with some twenty minutes remaining, Mark Bright settled the affair. A Palace raid down our left caused confusion, then chaos in Oldham's ranks. John Salako centred, Ian Wright won a header and Bright thumped an emphatic volley into the roof of the net from some five yards range.

Palace might have had more. John Hallworth made a string of saves to deny them, with Andy Gray frustrated more than once – the victory was certainly deserved. Intriguingly though, perhaps other Palace fans will agree that the details of the occasion were quickly forgotten in the wake of the startling news which so soon followed it.

Mark Bright notches Palace's winner at Oldham.

Oldham Athletic 2	Crystal Palace 3
Marshall	*Salako, Wright*
Holden	*Bright*

Saturday 2 November 1991   Football League, First Division
Referee: Mr T. Holbrook   Attendance: 34,231

Geoff Thomas's (centre) header flashes past the Liverpool defenders to gain Palace victory at Anfield.

Ever since Palace's 9-0 humiliation at Anfield, the Eagles and their followers have taken special relish in beating Liverpool. The semi-final defeat of the Reds was simply the first instalment in paying back the Merseysiders and this victory at their headquarters was another huge contribution towards restoring parity between the clubs in the minds of Palace supporters. It was also a fabulous demonstration of something they had sensed at the semi-final, then experienced at Selhurst Park the previous December; Liverpool's much vaunted supporters are not nearly so noisy or vocal as the northern media would have everyone suppose. Not for the first time they were found wanting by comparison with the massed ranks of three thousand Palace fans in the Anfield Road stand, who were in great voice, before, during and after the match and, even when the side was in arrears, continued to provide lusty encouragement, so that it represented the highlight of the entire 1991/92 season.

Much was being made at the time of Liverpool's lengthy injured list, but it should equally be noted that this outstanding result was achieved by a Palace team that lacked Andy Thorn, John Salako or Richard Shaw for the same reason, and that early in the second half they lost Andy Gray and Paul Mortimer, two of their most experienced players, in quick succession.

The teams entered Liverpool's famous arena to a barrage of noise, a balloon welcome from the Palace fans and in pouring rain, but with Eddie McGoldrick sweeping immaculately behind a defence that was tight and controlled, it was apparent from the early exchanges that either side might win. In fact, from about the half-hour mark, Palace began to assert themselves and to impose an authority upon Liverpool as their confidence grew, but just before half time burly

Liverpool 1   **Crystal Palace 2**
Hysen   *Gabbiadini*
                        Thomas

LIVERPOOL v. CRYSTAL PALACE

Bruce Grobbelaar did not feel too happy by the end of the afternoon!

Swedish international Glenn Hysen headed his side in front, following a left side corner.

Palace may have lacked a little in ambition earlier in the game but they scarcely deserved to be in arrears and the interval discussion in the dressing room inspired a new sense of purpose and direction so that, playing towards the Kop, Palace took the second half to their hosts with a display of passion, character and no little skill. The Liverpool defence, which had been uneasy all afternoon, soon paid the price: six minutes after the restart, Marco Gabbiadini scythed the ball past Bruce Grobbelaar from close range to restore the status quo following a first class move down the right flank which involved four other players and culminated in a low cross from near the corner flag from overlapping full back Gareth Southgate.

From then on, the destiny of the points was never really in any doubt as Palace, providing compelling entertainment and in spite of losing experienced men to injuries, continued to attack the bewildered Reds, whose fans were unable to raise their team's wilting perfor-mance. To the mounting enthusiasm, anticipation and realisation among Palace's packed supporters, the Eagles reshuffled – and dominated the home side so thoroughly that, when they scored again in the 72nd minute, when a right-side corner was flicked on by Eric Young then headed into the net by Geoff Thomas, the goal was actually long overdue!

Liverpool, naturally, roused themselves, but to a crescendo of deafening sound from the splendid Palace support, the Palace men held off the Reds' rally with tenacity and even aplomb. The Palace programme team dubbed the Liverpool conquerors 'The Anfield Avengers' and there was no doubt that this success was one of the greatest Palace victories. And, for those of us who had also been present at the 0-9 defeat of two seasons before, it was a marvellous, unforgettable, ecstatic occasion.

Liverpool: Grobbelaar, Jones, Burrows, Hysen, Molby (sub Rosenthal 78), Tanner, Saunders, Houghton, Rush, Ablett, McMahon.
Crystal Palace: Martyn, Southgate, Sinnott, Gray (sub Pardew 55), Young, Humphrey, Mortimer (sub Rodger 54), Thomas, Bright, Gabbiadini, McGoldrick.

CRYSTAL PALACE v. BLACKBURN ROVERS

Saturday 15 August 1992
Referee: Mr R. Milford

FA Premier League
Attendance: 17,086

Palace's first opponents in the Premiership were Blackburn – the very club they had deprived of top-flight status in the 1989 play-off final over three years before. However, Rovers had made huge investments from the personal fortune of local steel magnate Jack Walker in the interim and had at last gained the promotion they craved. Their team building and financial outlay continued during the close season, with the arrival of England striker Alan Shearer their most audacious and costly signing.

For the Palace there was a totally familiar look to the side Steve Coppell selected. With the sole exception of John Salako, the line-up was entirely composed of men who had appeared for the club in the closing stages of 1991/92.

Although a posse of photographers from the national daily and Sunday papers were lined up at the Whitehorse Lane end in anticipation of Alan Shearer's exploits, Palace's ace goalscorer Mark Bright notched the ground's and the club's first ever Premier League strike, before our admiring Holmesdale Road supporters after a little more than half an hour. He reached a long cross from the left flank from Richard Shaw and sent a crisp downward header bouncing into the net out of the reach of Rovers' goalkeeper Bobby Mimms. Just before half time, Stuart Ripley replied for the visitors with a headed equaliser but, showing tremendous character against Rovers' expensively assembled stars, Palace forged ahead with just less than half an hour to play. A left-side corner was never properly cleared and when it was hoofed out to Gareth Southgate some twenty yards from goal, the youngster delivered a crashing right-footed volley into the top left-hand corner of the net with a shot that was still rising when it hit the stanchion.

Alan Shearer then proceeded to justify his enormous £3.6 million transfer fee and beat Nigel Martyn with two spectacular drives in a quarter of an hour (which to the mortification of Palace fans the media proceeded to show over and over again on our television screens), but Palace refused to submit and they replied with another fine goal deep into injury time. This goal owed everything to Palace's pair of youthful substitutes, Simon Rodger and Simon Osborn, who, in contrast to Blackburn's costly acquisitions, had cost us virtually nothing! Palace were awarded a free kick out on our right. Simon Rodger flighted it into the heart of Rovers' danger area and there was Simon Osborn, rising high to head a precise and thoroughly deserved equaliser.

The action against Blackburn was heated and intense!

Crystal Palace 3
Bright, Southgate
Osborn

Blackburn Rovers 3
Ripley
Shearer (2)

CRYSTAL PALACE v. LIVERPOOL

Wednesday 16 December 1992
Referee: Mr P. Foakes

Football League Cup, Fourth Round Replay
Attendance: 19,622

Palace had gained a deserved draw in the original tie at Anfield, where we had only been denied outright victory by a contentious penalty, so there was inevitably something of an atmosphere at Selhurst Park when the sides resumed the contest in this replay.

With a youthful line-up, the Eagles surrendered much of the early possession and territory, but they did so with confidence that Liverpool would find it difficult to assert their alleged superiority and in the belief that Palace would find them vulnerable to their breaks and at free kicks and corners. Sure enough, in an early Palace raid, Steve Nicol wildly sliced a Gareth Southgate cross narrowly over Mike Hooper's crossbar, but Palace snatched the lead immediately afterwards when Grant Watts headed in Simon Rodger's corner that had been flicked on to him by man of the match, Andy Thorn. However, as the half hour approached Liverpool got back on terms, although, perhaps inevitably, it came from another penalty – for which, as at Anfield – the reason was obscure. Mike Marsh converted the penalty to set up what was turning into an enthralling, if now extremely wet evening.

The balance of chances during the rest of ordinary time certainly favoured the Eagles, but once the match was into extra time, Palace's young side was quite superb. Early in the first half Palace were denied a possible penalty for obstruction by Rob Jones following a free kick but then, after 101 minutes' play, their pressure finally gained its reward. The Reds' skipper, Nicol, miskicked in attempting to bludgeon clear John Humphrey's forward ball into the Liverpool penalty area after a free kick. The ball looped high, up and over the stranded goalkeeper. Andy

Thorn saw the opening, loped in, rose and gleefully headed the dropping ball into the untenanted net from close range. The crowd and the Palace players went wild with delight and, when Liverpool's immediate riposte from Jamie Redknapp hit the crossbar and flew into the seething terraces, the Reds knew that they had little more to offer. Palace's victory was all the more praiseworthy because it was gained with a team where eight players were under twenty-five, and because Liverpool had been unable to score a single goal other than from the penalty spot in three and a half hours of football – and both the awards from which they profited were for offences which were not apparent to neutral observers in the press boxes.

Andy Thorn shows his delight after scoring the extra-time winner against Liverpool.

Crystal Palace 2
Watts
Thorn

Liverpool 1
Marsh (pen)

(after extra time)

CRYSTAL PALACE v. CHELSEA

Wednesday 6 January 1993
Referee: Mr K. Barrett

Football League Cup, Fifth Round
Attendance: 28,510

On a sodden Selhurst Park pitch, passed fit by the referee only half an hour before kick-off following an early evening deluge of rain, and in conditions thus made decidedly treacherous underfoot, Palace's enforced combination of experience and raw talent saw the club safely through to its first ever appearance in the semi-finals of the League Cup by beating their powerful London neighbours, Chelsea. Since Palace have been involved in this competition since its inception in 1960, cynics might argue that this achievement has been an awfully long time in coming! Indeed it has, but the manner of it will probably stay in the memories of those Eagles fans who saw it equally as long!

The match was played throughout in a continuous downpour and the resultant conditions were to have an effect upon the outcome with only five minutes gone. Eddie McGoldrick completed some skilful defending near the touchline and then sent a long, raking pass upfield. It reached the Blues' danger zone where Frank Sinclair inadvisedly attempted to play the ball back to his goal-keeper, only to watch in horror as it stuck, as if in glue, in a pool of water in the 'D' on the edge of the penalty area in front of the packed Holmesdale terrace. Chris Coleman showed great awareness and was able to reach the ball first by slithering through the mire and his left-footed shot passed the exposed 'keeper, then ran on towards the goal, slowly, agonis-ingly, and itself held back on the sodden turf, but in a bizarre piece of apparent slow motion, it retained sufficient pace to creep across the goal-line – although it stopped just a foot inside the goal and certainly never reached the netting. It was certainly one of the strangest goals ever witnessed!

Nigel Martyn made the first of many splendid saves that evening to deny Chelsea a

Chris Coleman.

Crystal Palace 3
Coleman
Ndah, Watts

Chelsea 1
Townsend

CRYSTAL PALACE v. CHELSEA

Grant Watts.

quick response, but he had no chance with the fine shot delivered by Blues' skipper Andy Townsend after 18 minutes, although Townsend's contribution to the evening was largely overshadowed by the Eagles' own midfield supremo, the ever-improving Geoff Thomas, who was by now really beginning to resemble the player who had won nine full England caps in the previous two years.

However, a little after half an hour, Palace were again in front. An Eddie McGoldrick free kick into the heart of Chelsea's goalmouth was flicked on by Eric Young, then retrieved at full stretch beyond the far post by Andy Thorn who, under pressure from an opponent, was able to put sufficient purchase on the ball to prevent Kevin Hitchcock from holding it. It skidded through the goalkeeper's hand into the path of the prowling young George Ndah, who adjusted his stride and then prodded the ball over the line from three or four yards for his first senior goal for the club.

Fellow teenager Grant Watts made another telling input to Palace's progress in this season's League Cup tournament three minutes after the interval. After the ball had crossed and re-crossed the Chelsea penalty area without effect, Simon Rodger, up from the back to press to home the attack, lofted it into the centre of the goalmouth towards which Grant was racing. He leant back, and, falling, lashed a left-footed killer blow into the bottom corner of the net as Hitchcock dived the other way.

Nigel Martyn protected Palace's lead impressively as Chelsea strove to find a route back into the contest, and he handled extremely well in those most testing of circumstances for a goalkeeper, with one double save midway through the second half providing particularly spectacular action for Palace fans to savour.

The end came amid wonderful crowd backing from our supporters. Many were drenched to the skin but all were delighted to have witnessed Palace's success, which had at least ended the long, long wait to reach the last four in this League Cup competition in such spectacular and emphatic fashion.

Crystal Palace: Martyn, Humphrey, Bowry, Coleman, Young, Thorn, Ndah, Thomas, Watts (sub Gordon 77), Rodger, McGoldrick.
Chelsea: Hitchcock, Clarke, Sinclair, Townsend, Lee, Donaghy, Stuart, Fleck (sub Spencer 75), Harford, Newton, Myers (sub Le Saux 54).

Saturday 28 August 1993	Football League, Division One
Referee: Mr P.S. Danson	Attendance: 14,428

Palace secured many fine victories on their way to the 1993/94 Division One championship, but this early season one was the occasion when The Eagles demonstrated that their relegation blues from the previous May had been dealt with and gave exciting advance notice of their credentials.

Pompey had gone close to promotion the previous season themselves, and a dazzling eight-pass move, which ended with a crisp angled drive past Nigel Martyn after only six minutes, revealed their pedigree to the silent disbelief of the Holmesdale Road faithful.

But Palace began to apply themselves to their task and, with the assistance of a misjudgement by Pompey's defender Andy Awford, they were on terms twelve minutes later. Awford sent a pass across his penalty area intended for 'keeper Barry Horne, but Bobby Bowry was on to it like a black cobra, intercepted, then slipped the ball to Chris Armstrong who netted on the rebound from close range after Horne had blocked his first effort. Almost a quarter of an hour later, and with the control of the game having been wrested from the increasingly physical visitors, the marauding Dean Gordon linked up with the attack, to put Palace ahead with a spectacular header from an accurate right side cross from Paul Williams, whose influence on our behalf was now increasing with every game.

After the interval Palace became dominant and the goal of the match was produced by Gareth Southgate soon after the hour. It was described by manager Alan Smith as 'one of the best goals you'll ever see' and certainly for sheer athleticism and awesome finishing it was in the highest class. Palace's vice captain won a tackle with Warren Neill well inside his own half and then drove forward with the ball in a run of sixty yards before unleashing a tremendous drive from some twenty yards which left the bemused goal-keeper absolutely helpless. It brought every Palace fan to his feet in delight and admiration and was the cue for lusty singing of a selection of Palace songs.

Totally confident now, Palace piled on the pressure and Chris Armstrong quickly added a fourth, moving onto a long cross-field pass from Dean Gordon, then bearing down on the 'keeper in a one-on-one with confidence and class oozing from every pore, before striking the ball past him. Chris crowned the proceedings with another picture goal to complete his first Palace hat-trick near the end with a supreme flying header from Bobby Bowry's cross.

Gareth Southgate receives due acclaim after his stunning goal.

Crystal Palace 5
Armstrong (3)
Gordon, Southgate

Portsmouth 1
Neill

MIDDLESBROUGH *v.* CRYSTAL PALACE

Sunday 1 May 1994
Referee: Mr A. Flood

Football League, Division One
Attendance: 8,638

David Whyte (part hidden) nets Palace's second strike at Middlesbrough with this header.

It was at Middlesbrough's Ayresome Park on May Day that the Eagles were first acclaimed as champions of the Football League as a result of the 3-2 victory they had gained, to the delight and with the backing of over a thousand of our travelling fans.

In fact, it was 'Boro who forged ahead midway through the first half when their full-back put in a shot which deflected off Eric Young to enter our net with poor Nigel Martyn completely wrong-footed by the interception. Stung, Palace retaliated with some style and to great effect. Firstly, a little before the half hour mark, Gareth Southgate rose on the edge of the six-yard area to send an elegant, glancing header across the face of the goal and into the net off the inside of the far post, from an inswinging Simon Rodger free kick near the corner flag on Palace's right. Then, six minutes later, David Whyte grabbed the lead for Palace to mark his recall to the starting line-up for the first time in almost six months. Chris Armstrong had won possession and made ground before shooting hard and high, 'keeper Steve Pears parried at full stretch, but the ball fell into the path of the eager Palace forward who was able to reach it with his head and steer it into the empty net.

The first half action continued, for with a couple of minutes remaining Paul Wilkinson placed a header inside Palace's far post from a 'Boro free kick, so that at the break honours were even and there remained everything still to play for.

However, come the 56th minute and Palace were ahead again with the goal that clinched the title. David Whyte had powered a half-volley straight at Pears which had been repelled at the expense of a corner on the left: from Simon Rodger's kick, Chris Armstrong rose in immaculate manner to send a terrific header past Pears' left hand, high into the net and onto the stanchion from some fifteen yards range. The effort was at a perfect angle for Palace's supporters to appreciate all its finest points and it was a fitting finale.

Nigel Martyn made one late save of high quality to deny Paul Wilkinson, but 'Boro's other attempts to break through were competently dealt with by Palace's defence so that as the end approached the supporters were in fine and confident voice. After the final whistle the Palace players went across the pitch to celebrate with them the fact that the much coveted championship had been duly and stylishly won.

Middlesbrough 2	Crystal Palace 3
Liburd	*Southgate, Whyte*
Wilkinson	*Armstrong*

Sunday 8 May 1994
Referee: Mr K. Barrett

Football League, Division One
Attendance: 28,749

This occasion was much, much more than merely a football match – it was turned by Palace supporters into a pageant and a party of massive proportions, for the Eagles' fans were celebrating the triumphant homecoming of the Division One championship, although there was poignancy too because the afternoon would mark the passing of the Holmesdale Road terracing which was to undergo redevelopment in order to provide accommodation in accord with the all-seater demands of the Taylor Report. It was packed to its full width and presented a wonderful spectacle, a riot of red and blue, a passionate demonstration of allegiance, laden with emotion that could be felt as well as seen.

Thousands of red and blue balloons were released as the teams entered the arena and the match was played throughout with the pitch littered with their debris. Without question, it was the most spectacular welcome ever accorded to a Palace team and such was the exuberance at this stage of the proceedings that a Mexican wave went round Selhurst Park several times during the opening minutes of the game. Playing towards the Holmesdale terrace for the last time, Palace sought to cruise to victory on the wave of euphoria, but it was evident in the opening stages that some of the participants were finding it difficult to concentrate in the cauldron of noise and passion that Selhurst Park had become. Nevertheless, John Salako tested Perry Digweed and then sent a drive skimming just over the bar before Gareth Southgate's run was only halted by Keith Dublin on the edge of the penalty area.

At the opening of the second half, Palace fans sought again to raise the team's performance and David Whyte powered a header over the bar, but now the celebrations became a little muted as Andy Hessenthaler beat Nigel Martyn with a twenty-five yarder. Palace brought on Bruce Dyer in the hope that he could unlock the defence of his former teammates, but the Hornets defended stoutly under considerable pressure. In the last ten minutes the fans again tried to lift the side. John Humphrey responded with a long drive that drifted just wide of the target, then Digweed palmed over an Eric Young header as the entire Watford team defended a Palace free kick within their own penalty area. But the final throw was to be theirs, for, with only three minutes left and in bright sunshine, Tom Mooney added to the Hornets' lead with a bobbling shot from ten yards.

A good natured pitch invasion at the final whistle delayed Palace's lap of honour, but eventually, and to everyone's delight, the stars of the season paraded the championship trophy with justifiable pride so that all the fans could join in the celebration.

*Skipper Gareth Southgate holds the
League Champions' Trophy.*

Crystal Palace 0

Watford 2
Hessenthaler
Mooney

Arsenal v. Crystal Palace

Saturday 1 October 1994   FA Carling Premiership
Referee: Mr M. Bodenham   Attendance: 34,136

By any criterion, Palace's first victory over Arsenal at Highbury in the League (in twelve attempts, to date) would surely be regarded as a 'classic' match and a fine achievement, but, as so often, readers will find that the context in which it was gained make it even more compelling because it was achieved against a side which contained Palace's former goalscoring ace, Ian Wright, who was eager to net his hundredth strike for the Gunners and thereby, he hoped, to silence the taunts of those Eagles fans who regarded him as a traitor. Its inclusion in this book is, therefore, quite inevitable.

In fact though, to Ian's chagrin, Palace's success this day was both glorious and emphatic. Indeed, it probably represented the pinnacle of Palace's performances under manager Alan Smith for, even if the Gunners were 'only' a mid-table side at the time of this defeat, they were the European Cup Winners' Cup holders and were managed by George Graham, whose sides have always been notoriously difficult to beat. Palace were, on the other hand, already struggling for their Premiership lives and had gone without a win this season in any competition.

Intriguingly though, throughout 1994/95, the Eagles were able to raise their game for major fixtures. This match proved to be the first (hugely welcome, but utterly unexpected) indication of such a talent, and as the season progressed it provided the club with several further exciting pages for readers here to savour. But, if all of them were special, this one was absolutely wonderful – remember that it had been at Highbury that Palace had been relegated from the top flight in May of the previous year. Here they were again and, if the subsequent Cup successes of 1994/95 were thoroughly impressive, this match and this result will always be the one which Palace fans of the period – especially those who actually witnessed it – will regard as the season's outstanding highlight.

John Salako is en route to steer home Palace's second goal at Highbury.

Arsenal 1   **Crystal Palace 2**
Wright   *Salako (2)*

George Ndah's control prevents Paul
Davis from gaining possession.

Salako powers towards the Arsenal goal.

Equally, a glance at the Eagles players who achieved this result will demonstrate that it was brought about by a side which included several men whom few fans would rank among the greatest Palace stars. Yet on this occasion each one of them reached levels of performance that, frankly, made them unrecognisable, such is the magic of the game we love!

Palace's chief executioner on this dull and drizzly afternoon was John Salako, who, playing as a striker, scored both Palace's goals precisely upon the third anniversary of the terrible cruciate ligament injury he had sustained in a top flight match at Selhurst Park against Leeds United. How the enclave of Eagles fans cheered their favourites and derided their Arsenal counterparts as the home side struggled then failed to match our verve, enthusiasm and skill.

Salako was playing alongside Chris Armstrong and the lithe, twinkling duo made Arsenal's big defenders, Tony Adams and Andy Linighan, appear statuesque, and both of our goals were delightful affairs. Midfielder Bobby Bowry set up the first after nineteen minutes with a ball winning tackle that allowed Armstrong a clear run at goal. The pacy striker brushed past Linighan before shooting against the far post in front of the North Stand leaving John Salako a simple tap-in task. Shortly before half time a superb pass from skipper Gareth Southgate found Armstrong in acres of space on the right flank and his low, scudding cross was swept home gratefully and gracefully.

Ian Wright was able to head a consolation goal for his new employers, but the day was eventually Palace's amid a tension that was palpable, while the occasion was particularly sweet for those Palace fans who over the years had witnessed many severe maulings for our team at the imposing north London ground.

Arsenal: Seaman, Dixon, Linighan, Adams, Winterburn, Selley, Davis (sub Campbell 45), Schwarz, Merson, Wright, Smith.
Crystal Palace: Martyn, Patterson, Coleman, Shaw, Gordon, Southgate, Newman, Bowry, Salako, Armstrong, Ndah.

CRYSTAL PALACE v. MANCHESTER CITY

Wednesday 11 January 1995   Football League Cup, Fifth Round
Referee: Mr M. Bodenham   Attendance: 16,668

A second-half performance that was quite magnificent enabled the Eagles to blast four goals past toiling Manchester City and thereby claim their place in the League Cup semi-finals for the second time in three years. The night was bitterly cold but the match drew an expectant crowd who were treated to an opening quarter of fierce, intense action that was played at a furious pace. Even at this stage it was Palace who were creating more openings and George Ndah was a constant threat to the visitors on the left flank. City's greatest danger was posed through the power of German striker Uwe Rosler allied to the towering Niall Quinn, but Palace's central defensive duo of Richard Shaw and Chris Coleman had an outstanding game and nullified their opponents' best efforts.

It took the Eagles an hour to make their undoubted territorial advantage count, but then, against the backdrop of the gaunt, growing skeleton of the new Holmesdale Road stand, they struck with awesome style. A precisely weighted ball from the halfway line by Dean Gordon sent John Salako scurrying to the by-line and Andy Dibble could only palm away the cross. It fell for Gareth Southgate, who laid it back for Darren Pitcher to look up, aim and then fire into the untenanted top right corner of the net from sixteen yards for his first goal for our club. That hard earned but thoroughly deserved lead was then protected in supreme style by a goal-keeping save of utter brilliance by Nigel Martyn nine minutes later, when the England star swooped to his left to tip a Steve Lomas header around the post. Nigel had denied Gary Flitcroft equally effectively in a one-on-one just before the interval and the Palace 'keeper had an immaculate game.

With ten minutes remaining, the Eagles doubled their lead with a spectacular strike: George Ndah cleared a City corner to Chris Armstrong who saw John Salako already pacing away down the right. John took the pass, dribbled to the edge of the penalty area, turned inside Terry Phelan, then rasped a left-footer into the far top corner of the net to bring the crowd to its feet again! Palace's third goal four minutes later was a sheer delight. Gareth Southgate clipped a nonchalant ball to Chris Armstrong on the Eagles' right with the outside of his right boot and the Palace striker cut diagonally into the penalty area before unleashing a fierce, rising, right-footed shot across the diving Dibble and high into the rigging from some twelve yards but at a most acute angle. The finale came with just three minutes remaining: Dean Gordon and John Salako combined with foot and head respec-tively to open matters up for substitute Andy Preece to crash home left-footed from within the D to complete the annihilation.

A 'brotherly' cuddle in midfield during Palace's big win over Manchester City!

Crystal Palace 4   Manchester City 0
Pitcher, Salako
Armstrong, Preece

WOLVERHAMPTON WANDERERS v. CRYSTAL PALACE

Wednesday 22 March 1995
Referee: Mr G. Willard

FA Challenge Cup, Sixth Round Replay
Attendance: 27,458

Darren Pitcher.

Palace forgot their troubles in the Premier League by putting on a stirring, barn-storming performance in this FA Cup sixth round replay against powerful First Division Wolves at Molineux in front of a noisy, partisan crowd largely comprised of Black Country fans, and scored four marvellous goals to emphasise their seniority and avenge a third round dismissal at this venue the previous year.

The first goal came a little after half an hour: a John Salako throw-in on the right, level with the edge of the penalty area, was backheaded by Iain Dowie at the near post for Chris Armstrong to twist away from his marker on the perimeter of the goal area. Then, with his back to goal, he delivered a spectacular, right-footed bicycle kick into the right hand side of the target. But Wolves' reply was almost immediate: a wickedly deflected cross from their right wrong-footed Palace's defensive cover and Eire international David Kelly was able to head past Nigel Martyn.

However, within three minutes the Eagles were ahead again with another fine-looking strike. Again, it sprung from a John Salako throw-in on the right. This one was back headed by Darren Patterson into the heart of Wolves danger zone and then knocked on by Ian Cox. Iain Dowie took the pace off the ball with his head, then swivelled and crashed the ball past the exposed Mike Stowell on the volley, right footed, from seven yards.

It was with half time imminent that the tie swung emphatically Palace's way and it did so with a goal of awesome power and execution. A high ball was blindly headed away by an increasingly desperate Wolves defence, but it fell straight to Darren Pitcher some twenty-five yards from goal. The Palace midfielder cushioned the ball with his chest and then slammed a left-footed half volley which soared high over the 'keeper before dipping into the right-hand angle of the crossbar and goalpost.

But the best goal of all was the climax to the evening midway through the second half. Man of the match Chris Armstrong latched onto a fine ball from Ian Cox on the right flank, and then accelerated past Brian Law on the outside of the edge of the penalty area before firing an awesome rising drive some three yards from the by-line and at an extremely acute angle between the goalkeeper and the near post. The ball ended up in the top far corner of the goal, where it lodged above the stanchion in the tension of the rigging.

It was a supremely fitting conclusion to an impressive Palace performance and a goal that was eminently suited to grace their entry into the FA Cup semi-finals for only the third time.

Wolverhampton Wanderers 1
Kelly

Crystal Palace 4
Armstrong (2)
Dowie, Pitcher

CRYSTAL PALACE v. MANCHESTER UNITED (at Villa Park)

Sunday 9 April 1995
Referee: Mr D. Elleray

FA Challenge Cup, Semi-Final
Attendance: 38,256

Chris Armstrong celebrates his
semi-final goal with Iain Dowie.

Palace had played their way into their third FA Cup semi-final and put on an enthralling display against their 1990 Cup Final opponents, Manchester United, which completely belied their lowly position in the Premier League. Boosted by the January arrival of Northern Ireland striker Iain Dowie and then that of Eire midfielder Ray Houghton in March, Palace were able to produce a performance which ranked alongside the 1990 one at this stage against Liverpool at the same venue, even if it did not quite achieve the same outcome.

An enthralling encounter of great skill and commitment ensued and for Palace fans at Villa Park, the only disappointment was that their reward was merely a replay. Palace were by far the better side before the break when Peter Schmeichel was certainly the busier 'keeper. Even his telescopic arms could not reach the ball in the 32nd minute when John Salako leapt high at the far post to head back a right-side cross from Chris Armstrong, and Iain Dowie was able to nod into the net from the closest possible range. United's first equaliser took a deflection from a free kick and the tie was into extra time before Chris Armstrong lobbed over Schmeichel from some fifteen yards, but United replied promptly and with neither side able to find a killer strike, a replay became necessary the following Wednesday.

However, it only became apparent on the morning after the game that Nigel Martyn had sustained a broken index finger on his left hand in a clash with David Beckham in only the second minute. Having played throughout in considerable pain, Martyn would now miss the replay, along with several games of the crucial run-in to the Premiership season.

Deprived of Nigel Martyn's talents, Palace looked to Rhys Wilmot to deputise. Rhys had joined the club at the start of the season from Grimsby in an £80,000 deal to provide cover for Martyn. However, he had only played three minutes of top-class football for Palace since the move. It was also necessary for Dean Gordon to replace Chris Coleman in the Eagles' starting line-up but, as in the 1990 Cup Finals between the clubs, while the first game had been a fiesta, the second was dour. Palace conceded two set-piece goals in the last quarter of an hour of the first half without reply, but the whole occasion was marred by the double sending off of United's shamed Roy Keane for stamping on Gareth Southgate and of Darren Patterson for retaliation.

Crystal Palace 2
Dowie
Armstrong

Manchester United 2
Irwin
Pallister

(after extra time)

CRYSTAL PALACE v. GRIMSBY TOWN

Tuesday 5 March 1996
Referee: Mr S.G. Bennett

Football League, Division One
Attendance: 11,548

Sometimes a match that is rather lacklustre in many ways can be illuminated by an individual performance of such brilliance that the whole occasion is electrified for everyone who is present. That was certainly the case at Selhurst Park on this early March evening when the Eagles' ace striker Dougie Freedman hit an amazing quick fire, first-half hat-trick against Grimsby Town to set Palace on their way to their best victory for some eight-and-half years, drive them towards their highest position in the table to date that season – that is, firmly within the play-off places – and to emphasise their increasing credibility as contenders for promotion back to the Premiership.

But there are other reasons too for eulogising about Dougie's terrific contribution – not only did it represent Palace's hundredth League and Cup hat-trick since the club joined the Football League in 1920 but it was then – and remains – the Eagles' fastest in this department in their entire history since it all took place in just eleven minutes.

Dougie's opener was a cracking volley from a massive David Hopkin long throw, while the second, emanating from precisely the same source, was a fierce low drive. Only a minute afterwards Dougie lashed his third from close range after George Ndah's header from a Marc Edworthy cross had rebounded off the bar.

The avalanche continued and the match was still inside its opening half hour when Hopkin himself collected an easy goal – his ninth of the term – but there was to be no respite for the beleaguered Mariners as Ray Houghton drove upfield to slide a shot past the advancing goalkeeper. Palace fans in the Whitehorse Lane stand have seldom enjoyed a half more!

Inevitably, the Eagles eased off the pressure after the break and Grimsby did manage to hit both of Palace's uprights as they sought some consolation, but Palace supporters who were hoping for a goal riot were disappointed.

Palace boss Dave Bassett had the context and the summing up absolutely right in the post-match interview, agreeing that the match itself had not been one of the best and that the final scoreline was a flattering one. This was true enough – but those Palace fans who saw this superb example of an in-form striker's predatory skill will always savour the memories of that night.

Dougie Freedman.

Crystal Palace 5
Freedman (3)
Hopkin, Houghton

Grimsby Town 0

READING v. CRYSTAL PALACE

Saturday 21 September 1996
Referee: Mr S. Bennett

Football League, Division One
Attendance: 9,675

Now, I must admit, that this entry is pure indulgence! Of course, any six-goal spree by the Palace away from Selhurst Park would be a contender for inclusion in a book like this by any Eagles' fan, but for this author it is an absolute must! Firstly, it took place precisely upon the fiftieth anniversary of my Palace 'debut', with my dad on the Holmesdale Road terrace, behind the goal – I can still smell the grass and hear the players' shouts! But also hugely significant is where this game took place: Reading – the county town of the area where I work and have had my home for over twenty-four years; Reading – the one club to have put ten goals past the Palace in my lifetime…and didn't the west Berkshire undertakers remind me of it when all the local papers were featuring the fiftieth anniversary of that disaster a few weeks before this one! As Palace's goal tally at Elm Park mounted, I was a little boy again hearing that the team had lost 10-2 at a place called Elm Park, Reading. Now, here I was at that very venue seeing that defeat avenged in wonderfully comprehensive fashion. If we could only include ten Palace matches in this book, this one would have to be among them.

The day was also a special one for Palace goalkeeper Carlo Nash who was making his top class debut - in a most excellent fashion! He made a fine, early back-pedalling save but was then largely untroubled as the Eagles romped to a 5-0 lead within the hour, all the goals coming in less that thirty minutes either side of half time.

A niggling contest produced five bookings in the first twenty minutes, but then the goals began to flow. David Tuttle headed the opener on his local ground from an Andy Roberts cross after a left-side corner, and then Bruce Dyer won the ball and made the pass from which Dougie Freedman sidestepped Keith McPherson and then drove home, low past the goalkeeper.

Four minutes into the second half, Kevin Muscat's close-range header was his first in Palace colours and came from a Bruce Dyer cross. Dyer himself netted the fourth from a penalty awarded when Dougie Freedman was hauled down. Barry Hunter was dismissed for that foul and worse was to follow for the Royals when Carl Veart lobbed the goalkeeper for Palace's fifth goal.

Andy Roberts joined Hunter in the dressing rooms on the hour after receiving his second yellow card and Reading gained some consolation shortly afterwards from the penalty spot, but the last word lay with Palace and substitute George Ndah, who beat an opponent on the halfway line and then sped away to lift the ball over the advancing Mihaylov and complete one of the most satisfying afternoons I have ever spent as a follower of Crystal Palace.

David Tuttle.

Reading 1
Morley (pen)

Crystal Palace 6
Tuttle, Freedman, Muscat
Dyer (pen), Veart, Ndah

CRYSTAL PALACE v. WOLVERHAMPTON WANDERERS

Saturday 10 May 1997
Referee: Mr N. Barry

Football League, Division One Play-Off Semi-Final
Attendance: 21,053   (First leg)

Dougie Freedman receives congratulations after scoring his first goal.

Play-offs! Love them or loathe them, most genuine football fans agree or admit that they usually provide compelling entertainment – whether they produce heartache (as they must, inevitably, for three of the four clubs who become involved in them from each of the Football League Divisions, each year) or glory for the eventually successful, promoted club.

Palace's third entry into the play-offs (and the second one engineered by manager Steve Coppell) initially pitted them against Wolves. The Eagles had finished 1996/97 in sixth place in their division while the Black Country outfit had come third, five points ahead of us in the table, so that Palace's game was the first leg of the semi-finals. It was realistically expected to prove an extremely close affair because Wolves possessed the best away record in the division by a wide margin, so a Palace victory at Selhurst Park by any scoreline would be regarded as welcome and could prove conclusive because, curiously, Wolves were rather less effective at their own headquarters.

By a strange coincidence, Wolves' line-up included two former Palace mid-field favourites in the persons of our 1990 Cup Final skipper and England international Geoff Thomas along with the neat, clever, hardworking Simon Osborn. Both had given our club excellent service, but this afternoon was not the occasion for the slightest respect to be paid to old reputations! Also playing for Wolves – and to considerable effect – was a young man who was soon to join the staff at Selhurst Park and go on to represent Crystal Palace with great ability to an increasing level of distinction, the over-lapping full back Jamie Smith.

Like so many major footballing occasions, Palace's 1997 play-off match was bigger than the game the two sides were able to provide in the opening half. It was played largely in the rain, heavy at times, although the elements did ease as the interval approached, but these initial stages were tension-laden and dour. There was nothing to choose between the sides at the

Crystal Palace 3
Shipperley
Freedman (2)

Wolverhampton Wanderers 1
Smith

CRYSTAL PALACE v. WOLVERHAMPTON WANDERERS

Palace skipper Ray Houghton meets up with his predecessor Geoff Thomas!

break, but the songs and cheers of both sets of supporters were adding to the atmosphere.

It was just after the hour, in the strengthening sunshine, that Palace, now attacking their favoured Holmesdale Road end, achieved the breakthrough. Simon Rodger delivered an inswinging corner and Neil Shipperley climbed high to plant a downward header firmly into the net. That remained the scoreline until just two minutes to go, but there then erupted one of the most gripping and astonishing culminations to a game that Palace fans have ever witnessed, because there followed an extra-ordinary finale with three goals in the last two minutes which sent every fan who was present through the whole gamut of emotion.

First, Palace substitute Dougie Freedman extended the Eagles' lead with a vicious dipping volley from twenty yards which brought the Palace supporters to their feet as one man, only for Jamie Smith to net his first-ever goal for Wolves in reply to reduce his side's arrears. However, with the encounter now running into injury time, Palace restored their two-goal advantage with a glorious finale. A long free kick from Andy Roberts found Andy Linighan in an advanced position. The former Arsenal man headed the ball down for Dougie Freedman to flick a devastating lob over the exposed goalkeeper from some twelve yards – thereby providing one of those delightful ironies in which the game abounds! Dougie was unable to appear in the Wembley play-off decider, should Palace progress to that stage, due to an indiscretion against Port Vale in the final League match the previous weekend, but now he had propelled the Eagles into a position from which that likelihood was now intensely probable.

There was barely time for the ball to be respotted and for play to resume before the final whistle went…but it took rather longer for everyone's overstretched emotions to subside!

Crystal Palace: Nash, Edworthy, Gordon, Roberts, Davies, Linighan, Hopkin, Houghton (sub Veart 62), Shipperley, Dyer (sub Freedman 73), Rodger.
Wolverhampton Wanderers: Stowell, Smith, Thompson, Atkins, Williams, Curle, Thomas, Ferguson, Bull (sub Foley 85), Roberts, Osborn.

WOLVERHAMPTON WANDERERS v. CRYSTAL PALACE

Wednesday 14 May 1997
Referee: Mr C. Wilkes

Football League, Division One, Play-Off Semi-Final
Attendance: 26,403   (Second Leg)

The Eagles' second leg engagement at Molineux took place on a warm, sunny Black Country evening but Steve Coppell's pre-match disposition was anything but mellow as he chose to reinforce his defence in anticipation of the inevitable Wolves onslaught that was bound to materialise at some stage of the proceedings. Consequently, Kevin Muscat, who would sign for Wolves later in the year, was drafted in at the expense of Ray Houghton, while the experience of David Tuttle was preferred to the Welsh passion of Gareth Davies at the heart of the defence.

The changes proved highly beneficial in the face of almost constant Wolves pressure and in an atmosphere of unbridled hostility, so that Palace were able to cope well enough with the intense demands of the evening, though they conceded a Mark Atkins goal just after half an hour.

However, the overall situation swung Palace's way again in the sixty-sixth minute when the recently crowned Player of the Year, David Hopkin, scored a goal that was fully worthy of that award and showed all the pace, power and eye for goals that had drawn such attention from the Premiership's big clubs and would take him to Leeds during the summer. He beat two defenders and then the goalkeeper from the edge of the penalty area to tilt the affair Palace's way again, leaving Wolves needing two goals if they were to take the tie into extra time.

For a little while the volume at Molineux was coming from the Palace fans, but as the minutes ticked away so Wolves regrouped…and re-charged. With six minutes left, they had a corner on their right from which Adrian Williams headed past Carlo Nash and now there was a grandstand finish! The entertainment was riveting and even for those who were only watching, absolutely exhausting! But, even with generous added-on time, Wolves could not come again and Palace had secured a second Wembley final in successive years.

Watching the wild, jubilant carousal among the Eagles fans after the final whistle it was impossible to think of any Palace occasion when their supporters have celebrated in such fashion after seeing our team beaten!

David Hopkins evades a challenge
as he bears down on Wolves' goal.

Wolverhampton Wanderers 2
Atkins
Williams

Crystal Palace 1
Hopkin

(3-4 on aggregate)

CRYSTAL PALACE v. SHEFFIELD UNITED (at Wembley Stadium)

Monday 26 May 1997
Referee: Mr N. Barry

Football League, Division One Play-Off Final
Attendance: 64,383

Whenever Crystal Palace FC have appeared at Wembley Stadium the fans have made a major contribution towards the colour, pageantry and exuberance of the occasion. They did so even on Palace's Wembley debut – the often forgotten Football League Centenary tournament in April 1988 at which the old stadium was never more than a third full and when the club was by far the best supported of the sixteen participants – and they have done so ever since. But at this 1997 First Division play-off final they did so in a manner that was unique at the club, certainly extremely rare at even the most significant matches that Wembley has hosted and which certainly appeared to affect the ultimate outcome – details to be revealed shortly!

As at previous Palace spectaculars at Wembley, the Selhurst Park fans were there in force – some thirty thousand of us – to cheer the Eagles past this one last hurdle, in the shape of Sheffield United, and on, back into the Premiership. The now customary, carefully, cleverly orchestrated planning among the supporters ensured that the team was welcomed onto the arena with a riotous reception of noise and enthusiasm, with balloons in red and blue, coloured smoke, streamers and energetic movement. Frankly, other clubs may say how wonderful their support at big footballing events is: Palace fans have proved it time after time after time, putting their opposite numbers to shame in doing so, although it is curious to observe as fact that the media seldom make any mention of the supporters' contribution and that the television cameras virtually ignore it. As well as the inevitable tension generated by this (and every) play-off final, the players involved also had to contend with extreme heat and humidity and the temperature in the arena is reliably said to have exceeded 90 degrees Fahrenheit at its peak, as the game drew towards its conclusion.

Palace's opponents were Sheffield United, who had finished the League season one place above the Eagles in the table and had beaten play-off favourites for promotion Ipswich in their

semi-final. The Blades were managed by Howard Kendall, who was once allegedly considered for the Palace manager's job but is best remembered by Palace fans as the Everton boss who directly or otherwise consistently lamented the forceful approach Palace adopted, almost invariably with marked success, against the Toffees.

Once an early moment of danger from United's Petr Katchouro had been dealt with by Carlo Nash, Palace settled more quickly and certainly had the better of the first half but matters were much more even after the

Blades' David Holdsworth 'hangs on' to David Hopkins at Wembley.

Crystal Palace 1
Hopkin

Sheffield United 0

David Hopkin (centre) shares a moment or two with loyal Palace fan Colin Duncan and his son Ivor. (picture by Don Madgwick Jnr.)

break. Chances however, were few and both sides were at their most dangerous from set pieces. Then, with some ten minutes to go, an amazing thing happened, something possibly unique at Wembley and definitely a rarity there. The ranks of Palace's red and blue army of fans began to clap, sing, chant and cheer in unison to compelling effect. Perhaps twenty different Palace fans have claimed to have been the inspiration for this…and there is nothing to say that it sprung from a single source. It proved hugely emotional for Eagles fans present, while its effect upon the players was at least uplifting and, perhaps, match-winning.

The game reached its penultimate minute and its decisive moments when, playing towards the massed legions of their own fans, Palace gained a corner on the right. Andy Roberts played the ball short for Simon Rodger to put over an in-swinger with his trusty left boot. The Blades' Carl Tiler headed it away from above the penalty spot, but it fell to David Hopkin, standing unmarked some 22 yards out from goal to the left of the 'D'. David controlled the ball with his left foot, transferred it to his favoured right, looked up, adjusted his balance, aimed, then unleashed a stunningly spectacular strike that was fit to settle any showpiece at the famous stadium. The ball curled round and over the United rearguard, then dipped into the right hand corner of the net, leaving Simon Tracey merely a spectator and bringing an eruption of sound from the supporters as every Palace person in the arena leapt from their seats, punching the air in joy and relief.

Crystal Palace: Nash, Edworthy, Gordon, Roberts, Tuttle, Linighan, Hopkin, Muscat, Shipperley, Dyer, Rodger.
Sheffield United: Tracey, Holdsworth, Tiler, Nilsen, Spackman (sub Walker 90), White, Hutchison (sub Sandford 45), Ward, Whitehouse, Fjortoft, Katchouro (sub Taylor 25).

NORWICH CITY v. CRYSTAL PALACE

Saturday 3 April 1999
Referee: Mr A. Hall

Football League, Division One
Attendance: 16,754

Dean Austin's goal gave Palace victory at Norwich.

The previous match report referred to a spontaneous outburst of support for the Crystal Palace team from the Eagles' fans during the Wembley play-off final of 1997. Whether it was beneficial to their cause is difficult to evaluate dispassionately, although it seems likely that it was. But there has been another occasion when almost unbelievable support has been demonstrated which made the match at which it took place not only a 'classic' one for those Eagles folk who were part of and present at it, but also caused it to become totally unforgettable.

In several ways it was different from the Wembley phenomenon. This time it was most certainly organised; it was acknowledged by the Palace players to have been hugely effective; and it was aimed at very much more than simply seeking to win a football match, however important that may be. Two years on from the Wembley scenario and Crystal Palace FC had once more contrived to turn triumph into imminent disaster and there was no doubt that the club was in real peril. The Palace supporters had watched in amazement and dismay as the club's financial predicament deteriorated towards complete chaos. Star players were sold off to raise money to repay debts – forty-six members of the office staff were made redundant; and the remaining players were asked to accept a 'voluntary' forty per cent cut in their wages.

This Easter Saturday trip to Carrow Road fell just a few days after Palace had inevitably – many would add 'belatedly' – been put into the legal state of 'administration', and was seized upon by the supporters as an opportunity to express their allegiance to the club along with their disgust towards those who were conceived to be mainly responsible for the club's astonishing plight. The support offered to the makeshift team was almost beyond belief in the circumstances, both in numbers (well over two thousand) and of the noise generated. Admittedly, the low roof of Norwich's south stand into which the fans had been herded provided a perfect acoustic sounding board but even so it was exceptional.

All this forged a bond between the players and the fans – to which the team responded wonderfully. Although one of the remaining 'veterans', Dean Austin, secured the decisive strike with a downward, unmarked header as early as the thirteenth minute, Palace had four youthful debutants at Norwich and seven teenagers involved! 3-0 would actually have been a more fitting scoreline too, given that Clinton Morrison and Andrew Martin both hit the City woodwork. Manager Steve Coppell rightly called the teams display 'magnificent', but it was due in no small degree to the inspiration it was able to draw from the equally superb support provided by the fans. The scenes at the final whistle almost defy words. Having bayed for the end for several minutes, the Palace section erupted into unrestrained delight when it came. Players and fans saluted each other – at one in adversity and with a battle deservedly won…together.

Norwich City 0	Crystal Palace 1
	Austin

Wednesday 1 November 2000
Referee: Mr R. Pearson

Football League Cup, Third Round
Attendance: 12,965

As earlier articles in this book have already shown, Palace manager Alan Smith had inspired the club to several impressive victories in Cup ties in his previous tenure as manager. The next few pages will demonstrate that he hadn't lost that talent by the time of his reappointment for 2000/01.

The Football League Cup provided Alan and his team with their first opportunity to claim a Premiership scalp. They had beaten Cardiff and Burnley, each over two legs, to reach the round in which the top-flight entrants became engaged and the draw took Palace to Filbert Street, the home of the League Cup holders Leicester City who had recently topped the Premier League and were managed by former Palace star Peter Taylor. Few folk away from Selhurst Park could see the Eagles surmounting this hurdle because by now the League Cup was a one-off knock-out: it would be decided on the night, going into extra time or even penalties if necessary.

'Decided' it most emphatically was, and with over a third of the game still to be played, but not in the way anyone, except, in all honesty, the most committed Palace fans, could have foreseen. What transpired in rather less than an hour produced the shock outcome of the season to date because the Premiership side was comprehensively beaten, while Palace, appearing here on the back of no fewer than six Division One defeats and one draw, were full value for their own outstanding victory.

Palace's opener, a little after a quarter of an hour, making it clear to everyone that the Eagles were present to compete seriously for a fourth round berth, was a

Andrejs Rubins' stunning strike ensured Palace's success over Premiership side Leicester at Filbert Street.

Leicester City 0

Crystal Palace 3
Morrison
Thomson, Rubins

Hayden Mullins was exceptional against Leicester.

sweet affair, stemming initially from a long corner from Wayne Carlisle. Full back Craig Harrison nodded it back at the far post and Clinton Morrison despatched it with his head from four yards.

Six minutes later it became apparent that Leicester were in deep trouble when Steven Thomson scored with a delightful 25-yard shot and had matters remained at 2-0 Steven would have been fêted by the media for his effort. But even this wonderful goal was surpassed by Palace's third, just seven minutes after the break. Leicester, in some desperation, had made three substitutions upon the resumption after the interval, but the moment which will live forever in the minds of all Palace fans and settled the outcome beyond all dispute, came from the slight figure of our Latvian international winger, Andrejs Rubins, a £2million October acquisition from Skonto Riga. Andrejs began a run with the ball at his feet from within the Palace half. Bought at least partly for his electrifying pace, Andrejs was in no danger of being caught by the pursuing Neil Lennon, but some thirty yards out he spotted the opening left by the advancing Simon Royce and unleashed a venomous drive that no goalkeeper on earth could have saved. It flew into the top left-hand corner of the net, completely stunned the Leicester men and reduced their token, face-saving efforts to mere formalities.

One quibble remains from that night with Palace fans. Palace completed a wonderful and unexpected victory at a high-ranking Premiership club, but this fact was virtually ignored by the television coverage of the round, while Andrejs' goal, certainly worthy of contention for 'Goal of the Season', was scarcely even screened again.

Leicester City: Royce, Rowett, Gilchrist (sub Elliott 46), Davidson, Sinclair, McKinlay, Gunnlaughson, Lennon, Guppy, Creswell (sub Benjamin 46), Edie (sub Izzett 46).
Crystal Palace: Kolinko, Mullins, Smith, Austin, Harrison, Carlisle, Thomson, Rodger, Black, Rubins, Morrison.

CRYSTAL PALACE v. TRANMERE ROVERS

Tuesday 28 November 2000
Referee: Mr D. Laws

Football League Cup, Fourth Round
Attendance: 10,271

This League Cup tie was the second meeting between the two clubs at Selhurst Park within ten days. Both sides had suffered injuries to key players in the interim, but the outcome again finished with a victory for Crystal Palace, albeit by an even narrower margin that the Division One game when the Eagles had scored two late goals to gain success after trailing 2-1 for most of the proceedings.

With a place in the last eight at stake, perhaps it was inevitable that the only all-Division One tie would be dour, uncompromising and keenly contested. Some pundits rued what they felt was a lack of quality to the proceedings: the fans of Palace and Tranmere would simply point these pompous fellows to the fact that both their clubs had dismissed high-riding top flight outfits, who, presumably, might be regarded as possessing the right sort of quality, in the previous round!

But without question, the contest provided gripping entertainment for the partisans who supported the two outfits involved. Although chances inevitably increased as the match proceeded, they generally were rare, but some disappointing finishing allied to excellent goal-keeping throughout contrived to take the tie into extra time and then into a penalty shoot-out with the scoresheet still blank.

Eagles skipper Dean Austin won the toss for choice of ends for the penalty saga, so the Holmesdale faithful were treated to a close-up view of this cruellest form of footballing action.

The standard of penalty taking was extremely high from both sides, but the Eagles were never in arrears in the shoot-out. The duel had proceeded to 4-4 from ten kicks when late Palace substitute twenty-year-old Andrew Martin, appearing after a long lay-off with a knee injury, netted Palace's fifth penalty with the best effort so far. Paul Rideout replied with a thoughtful low response; both goalkeepers then saved well and nineteen-year-old Stephen Kabba, another extra-time substitute, jinked up to tuck his kick low inside the left-hand post. And with the pressure now firmly upon him, and to a crescendo of noise from the Palace fans all around the ground, Reuben Hazell blasted the last kick of the game high into the delighted and relieved denizens of the Holmesdale Stand.

Thus, both the 1999/2000 winners and the beaten finalists in this competition had been put out of the 2000/01 competition by the Eagles. Palace had reached the quarter-finals of the League Cup for the first time in six years and the game, which had not finished until 10.30pm exactly, was the latest conclusion to a Palace fixture at Selhurst Park.

The Palace players celebrate their penalty shoot-out win over Tranmere.

Crystal Palace 0

Tranmere Rovers 0   (after extra time)

Palace won 6-5 on penalties

CRYSTAL PALACE v. SUNDERLAND

Tuesday 19 December 2000
Referee: Mr A. Wiley

Football League Cup, Fifth Round
Attendance: 15,492

The 2000/01 season was ultimately to become one of decline, anxiety and near disaster for Crystal Palace FC, but it was also one which provided several sensational and well-deserved victories over leading Premiership outfits. The Eagles were in fact to be seen at their best in the middle months of the season and in the League Cup, so that now, in the week before Christmas and with the competition into its quarter-final stage, the club were about to gain another spectacular success over powerful, illustrious and much-vaunted opponents.

Curiously, this meeting between Palace and Sunderland occurred just a few days after the FA Cup third round draw had paired the two clubs to meet at the Stadium of Light early in the new year. But perhaps more significant in the setting for this contest at Selhurst Park was the fact remarked upon in an earlier match account, that the later stages of the Football League Cup were decided in a single contest, so that Sunderland could not come to the Palace, shut up shop, play and settle for a draw, then aim to progress via a victory at their own headquarters. (Actually, the futility of such an approach was revealed when Palace themselves held the mighty Wearsiders at their superb new stadium in the FA Cup match less than three weeks later, but that was all in the future at the time of Sunderland's arrival for this League Cup tie.)

They did so with all the confidence and lustre of a top six Premiership outfit, but whether or not because they had chosen to rest three senior players, they never appeared to be of a calibre any different to the better of Palace's Nationwide League opponents, while the outcome was certainly not so advantageous to them as it all too often was to our Division One opponents! Bluntly, Sunderland always looked vulnerable to Palace's all action display and never appreciated the intensity of the Eagles' pressuring tactics. Palace had the clearer chances throughout the evening, although both goalkeepers saved superbly at times, notably Thomas Sorensen getting a hand to a goalbound shot from Clinton Morrison early in the proceedings and Alex Kolinko tipping a fierce drive from Julio Arca over the crossbar.

The Eagles led early in the second half in

Clinton Morrison – Man of the Match.

Crystal Palace 2	Sunderland 1
Forssell	*Rae*
Morrison	

Fan Zhiyi was superb at the heart of the Eagles' defence.

which they were playing towards the fans in the Holmesdale Road stand. A dreadful goalkick by Sorensen was seized upon by Morrison who veered to the left of the penalty area then unselfishly squared a low cross for Mikael Forssell to side foot into the gaping net with delight...only for Sunderland to regain parity just twenty-nine seconds later! Daniel Dichio headed down a cross from Darren Williams for Alex Rae to slip under Kolinko.

Now, at last, Sunderland demonstrated some willingness to match the tempo Palace had dictated for the game, but as the hour approached Palace were twice denied the lead within a minute by the woodwork. Forssell shrugged off two challenges then slammed a rising drive against the bar and moments later Clinton Morrison hit the bar from a Tommy Black cross.

But Sunderland's reprieve was only temporary and lasted just twenty minutes. Kolinko saved well from the subdued Kevin Phillips but in the 82nd minute the man of the match won it for Palace: Clinton Morrison beat Emerson Thome twice in the box then flashed a low, right-footed drive across the face of Sorensen's goal and into the bottom left-hand corner to ensure a third Palace appearance in the League Cup semi-finals and the proper result on the night at Selhurst Park. Amidst the euphoria in the stands, Morrison was engulfed by his delighted colleagues and manager Alan Smith ran to the touchline to embrace Palace's inspirational skipper Dean Austin.

The comments of Sunderland's manager, Peter Reid, after the game were salutary. 'The team that won had the greater desire and the better attitude' he declared. 'We were second best all over the pitch'. But what Mr Reid did not say was that his players would be very much better prepared mentally and hugely more effective thereby should they find themselves in similar circumstances again, and he demonstrated his own ability as motivator and manager when the Black Cats returned to Selhurst Park the following month and won a gripping FA Cup third round replay in extra time.

Crystal Palace: Kolinko, Smith, Austin, Zhiyi, Ruddock, Rodger, Mullins, Pollock, Black (sub Thomson 86), Morrison (sub Carlisle 89), Forssell.
Sunderland: Sorensen, Williams, Varga, Thome, Gray, Kilbane, Rae, Schwarz (sub Oster 81), Arca (sub McCann 56), Dichio, Phillips.

CRYSTAL PALACE v. LIVERPOOL

Wednesday 10 January 2001
Referee: Mr U. Rennie

Football League Cup, Semi-Final, First Leg
Attendance: 25,933

Palace's quarter-final League Cup success over Sunderland secured a two-legged semi-final against Liverpool and the Eagles drew a capacity crowd to their headquarters for their tie against Merseyside's five-time winners of the competition and the favourites to do so again. However, the pundits' judgement in these matters was certainly made to appear grandiose in the extreme in this first leg as the Reds were forced to pay a heavy price for their profligate finishing and Palace sent their fans home delighted by an inspiring victory.

The evening was raw and blustery and Palace were perhaps surprised by the manner in which Liverpool matched their early pace, and the visitors set up golden chances for Michael Owen and Emile Heskey in the first quarter of the game which both England aces spurned. From that point, however, the contest turned in Palace's favour – Westerveldt did brilliantly well to parry a Clinton Morrison drive when the Palace striker took a pass from Mikael Forssell and demonstrated that the Division One outfit were by no means overawed and had the potential as well as the confidence to surprise the Premier League sophisticates.

After the break the Eagles owed a considerable debt to Latvian international goalkeeper Alex Kolinko who made several excellent saves, but the Reds then had no immediate answer to Palace's passion or our two magnificent goals. Eleven minutes after the restart Palace's other Latvian international star, winger Andrejs Rubins drove a searing left-footed shot from the edge of the penalty area high into the net leaving Westerveldt helpless and bringing the entire Holmesdale Road stand to its feet as one man, then, some twenty minutes later, after a period of the most intense Palace pressure, Mikael Forrsell controlled a left-side cross from Craig Harrison for Clinton Morrison to hammer a right-footed rising drive into the top corner of the netting.

Jamie Smith is about to embrace Clinton Morrison after the striker had doubled Palace's lead.

Crystal Palace 2	Liverpool 1
Rubins	*Smicer*
Morrison	

Dean Austin knows too much for Liverpool's Emile Heskey.

But Liverpool were able to save themselves from utter humiliation by producing a classy response. The Reds showed their pedigree at last by responding almost immediately, substitute Vladimir Smicer side footing a by-line cross from debutant Jari Litmanen past Kolinko to keep his new club in contention with the second leg at Anfield to follow, although Palace's victory here was both deserved and one for the fans to savour so that the 'Glad All Over' anthem was blasted out into the night with unfettered joy at the conclusion of the contest.

Admittedly, the sequel to this highest peak of Palace's 2000/01 season was embarrassing on the pitch at Anfield, for Liverpool had been angered by their defeat at Selhurst, as well as by untimely remarks to the media made by some Palace players in the heat of the excitement of their stunning victory. But Palace's heavy defeat in the second leg cannot be allowed to take away anything from the glorious triumph which is the focus of this article and which ensures that all Palace fans will be eagerly awaiting Liverpool's next visit whenever that may be.

Crystal Palace: Kolinko, Mullins, Austin, Zhiyi, Harrison, Smith, Thomson, Rodger, Rubins, Forssell, Morrison.
Liverpool: Westerveldt, Babbel, Henchoz, Hyypia, Carragher, Barmby (sub Hammann 80), Biscan. Gerrard, Murphy (sub Smicer 64), Owen (sub Litmanen 64), Heskey.

STOCKPORT COUNTY v. CRYSTAL PALACE

Sunday 6 May 2001
Referee: Mr A. Leake

Football League, Division One
Attendance: 9,782

Wonderful as Palace's victories over top-flight League Cup opponents had been, it has to be admitted that our 2000/01 season went into steep decline after they were over. So swift was our deterioration that as the finale approached there grew the genuine possibility that we could be relegated back to the lower divisions for the first time since 1977. Thus, after Palace's defeat by Wolves in their final home game, manager Alan Smith was dismissed and replaced by that huge favourite at Selhurst Park Steve Kember. Steve immediately inspired a splendid 4-2 win at Portsmouth in the penultimate match, but, faced with a last day of the (League) season trip to Stockport, it was essential to win again, because the other candidates for the drop, Pompey, Huddersfield and Grimsby, all had home fixtures, although not necessarily straightforward ones.

Early in the proceedings Portsmouth and Grimsby had scored, and whilst Birmingham had gone ahead at Huddersfield, the Terriers had levelled, only for the Blues to lead once more. So with the interval score blank, Palace went in at half time occupying the fatal third relegation place. Tense? Of course it was tense – but it was going to become much more so!

With half an hour of the second half gone, Portsmouth had powered to a substantial 3-0 lead so were clearly safe. But the other scores were unchanged, so emotions among the Palace faithful at Stockport and those at home glued to radios and teletexts, were now stretched to the limit. Palace needed to score, but the minutes were ticking away all too quickly and the expressions on the faces of the men in the dug-out were fraught in the extreme.

An Abraham Wilbraham shot rebounded from the near post and then the referee ignored what appeared to be a blatant handball by David Hopkin just inside the penalty area...but whilst Palace fans were breathing huge sighs of relief, the ball was being rapidly transferred towards the other goal, behind which most of the Palace fans were stationed. Dougie Freedman took possession some fifteen yards inside the Stockport half, drove forward with neat, darting control, then ran on into the penalty area, where he cut inside a defender before thrashing home a rising drive from some ten yards. Relief and euphoria abounded among the fans – but there were still three minutes of ordinary time, plus five more added on to be endured and the ordeal still wasn't over then because everyone had to wait for what felt like ages before it was finally confirmed that Huddersfield had lost and that Palace were therefore safe.

The occasion has been dubbed 'The Great Escape' at Crystal Palace after the famous film, but certainly no one at Selhurst Park will ever want to experience a repeat of it!

Dougie's strike saved Palace at Stockport on the final day of the 2000/01 season.

Stockport County 0

Crystal Palace 1
Freedman